Celebrating the Earth is a series that reaches for rediscovery,
on the third planet from the sun, of the uniqueness there,
a uniqueness not only to celebrate, but also to savor.

There is but one ocean, although its coves have many names.
The single sea of atmosphere has no coves at all.
The miracle of soil, alive and giving life, lies thin
on the only earth, for which there is no spare.

In this series we seek a renewed stirring of love for that earth;
we plead that what man is capable of doing to it
is not always what he ought to do;
and we urge that all people now determine
that a wide spacious untrammeled freedom shall remain
to testify that this generation has love for the next.

Celebrating the Earth is about a different renaissance.
The old one came with discovery of new lands to exploit.
This new one comes with discovery of the earth's limits.

If, mindful of these limits, we learn new ways of perceiving
beauty and durability in the world, we may see that progress
is not the speed with which technology expands its control
or the rising number of things a man possesses,
but a process that lets man find serenity
and grow more content at less cost to the earth.

We shall welcome the inspiration of old masters and new.

CELEBRATING THE EARTH · A FRIENDS OF THE EARTH SERIES

Only a little planet, lines by Lawrence Collins and photography by Martin Schweitzer
Song of the Earth Spirit, by Susanne Anderson
Of all things most yielding, selections from Oriental literature by Marc Lappé, photographs by John Chang McCurdy

GENERAL EDITOR AND DESIGNER, DAVID R. BROWER

It is lovely indeed, it is lovely indeed. . . .

Song of the Earth Spirit

THE SNOWSTORM was over almost as fast as it began. We watched the thick layers of black cumulus blow apart and roll by. Transparent blue patches appeared and the sun broke through the somber sky. Rose Yellowhair bent forward and shielded her daughter, Charlene, from the cold wind. The rust of Rose's corduroy jacket and the turquoise of her satin-tiered skirt made a patch of brightness in the dark afternoon. Chestnut-colored sand blew across the desert and the sheep drifted toward the Yellowhair hogans in the distance.

A rainbow appeared against the deep clouds. Excitedly, I called Charlene, who was nine, to show her. I pointed at the rainbow. Rose Yellowhair came rapidly toward me, roughly shoved my arm away, and then hurried past me to urge the sheep on. In the two days I had known her she had been shy and gentle, speaking quietly in Navajo to me, though I did not speak that language. Clearly I had trespassed and had done something very wrong by pointing. I did not understand.

. . .

4]

Charlene came to me, took my hand and said solemnly, "It is bad for you to point at the rainbow. Evil spirits live there and they can travel down your arm and get in your body and you will get sick. If you want to point to a rainbow, turn your hand upside down and point with your thumb."

From Charlene on that visit I learned that I should try to avoid looking at lizards or insects, and certainly should never touch them. She didn't want to talk about why. I must never pull up any plants, but nobody would tell me the reason for that either. Natural phenomena and the earth seemed to play a very important part in every minute of Charlene's life, but in a spiritual way that she was reluctant to explain to an Anglo.

· · ·

For a long time, what I knew of Navajo life came to me in fragments. These made some things clearer, but they usually ended in deepening the mystery surrounding still others. I do not think I know now, or will ever understand very well who the Navajos are. The mystery will survive my curiosity, just as I think it has the inquiries of many others, even Navajos, who set out to understand the life of an entire people.

FRIENDS OF THE EARTH SAN FRANCISCO · NEW YORK · LONDON · PARIS

McGRAW-HILL BOOK COMPANY NEW YORK · ST. LOUIS · SAN FRANCISCO · TORONTO

Song of the Earth Spirit

by Susanne Anderson   edited, with a foreword, by David R. Brower

SUSANNE ANDERSON *considers herself largely self-taught. She went to art school in London but didn't pay much attention; at George Washington University, studying foreign affairs and political science, she become angry when her professor-advisor told her to study biology instead (she now thinks he was right). She got into photography when someone gave her a fourteen-year-old Nikon, still her favorite, and used for many of the photographs she made for this book. She was photography editor for* America Illustrated (*U.S.I.A.*), *has photographed for many national magazines and written for some, has won several photographic and art-director's awards, and has exhibited at the Corcoron Gallery (painting in the 'fifties, photography in 1972). She likes the work of Ansel Adams, Henri Cartier-Bresson, Wayne Miller, Eliot Porter, and Burk Uzzle. She, her attorney husband (and occasional editor), and her three daughters live in Washington, D.C.*

Mrs. Anderson hopes that a Navajo Friends of the Earth can be organized in Navajo country, run independently by Navajos just as the sister organizations of FOE are independently run in other countries—perhaps to be called NavaFOE for short. She is contributing a substantial share of her royalty from Song of the Earth Spirit *to help finance such an organization, and Friends of the Earth is matching her contribution.*

—D.R.B.

Publisher's note: This book is set in Centaur and Arrighi by Mackenzie & Harris, Inc., San Francisco. Color separations, lithography, and binding are by Arnoldo Mondadori Editore, Verona, on coated paper made by Cartiera Celdit and double-page collated and bound in Coloreta of Scholco. Lay out is by Kenneth Brower. Design is by David R. Brower.

Foreword

WHEN SOMEONE with roots in one culture wants to understand someone else with roots in another, there are traditional ways of trying, and anthropologists have used them long and well. There is also a way that develops if there is grace, openness, and love, and more and more people, especially young people, are exploring it. Only with such an approach, I think, could Song of the Earth Spirit happen, or could Susanne Anderson be able to capture the enduring moment — Ansel Adams's phrase — of the final photograph of the book.

It was the Navajo grandmother's eye that first caught mine. Other of Mrs. Anderson's black and whites spoke almost as clearly, and so did a color transparency or two. Could there be more color, and what would the text say? "This book," she replied, "should be a beautiful, sad, happy, powerful Navajo poem, not an Anglo sightseeing bus."

She has indeed kept out of the bus over the period of three years in which she spent many months with Navajos in a remote part of their land. Some were friendly, some hostile. Her daughter Sally had her eye blacked and her nose bloodied on her first day there, but didn't cry. Mrs. Anderson was invited, luckily, she says, into many Navajo homes. Even though she could not speak the language, she somehow got to be accepted. "I don't know the Navajo people," she hastens to explain. "I know a few Navajo people." For all her lack of science, or the limitations of being a stranger in original America, she got something genuine going, then kept in touch with people who had become close friends, visiting them on Black Mesa, talking to them frequently by telephone when she was back home. The photography moved well, but the text remained a problem until she learned the importance of keeping real names private, which this book does. Until then, she discovered, she had been allowed to approach only remotely what she could now hear, jot down, tape-record, and write about freely.

She did not, however, let complications make things complex, to which we owe much of the tenderness of her work. Her daughters took turns accompanying her, and their eyes helped hers. She took turns, too — herding sheep, "for day after day, and nothing happened. When a thunderstorm came, I would bring the sheep in." This is not how photographers usually work.

"I didn't have profound thoughts," she says. "I am a photographer, not an anthropologist, geologist, or botanist. I have become a friend of many Navajos, in the sense, I hope, that Navajos use the word. This book is really a story of our friendships. What it says is as true as I could write and photograph it. Still, the final product means far less to me than what happened to me in the process."

What happened to her can also happen to us, and beautifully. She has let us know about important little intimate human things that can last for millenia, and not be burned up in a mere century or two, leaving ashes in the wind.

Literal ashes, far too many, darken the Navajo sky. Our civilization, soaring to power by using up its environmental capital, now exports its power-plant pollution to what were the clean skies of the Southwest. To have taken the land was not enough; the air must be taken too, so that the Los Angeles basin, Central Arizona, and Las Vegas could force their roots out farther still, grow insatiably, and damn the expense as long as it wasn't theirs. And as long as it could be denied that there was a cost. I heard guides at the Four Corners and Black Mesa strip mines tell the same story as they excused the burial of soil aeons in the making under the dead rock that had lain over the coal they are converting to kilowatts and fly ash: "We are bringing new nutrients to the top."

This is an overachievement in creative PR that we can do without. One of the high costs of electricity is that it lets us see far too few stars. It is now taking the stars away from people who have barely enough electricity to let a scratchy tape recorder repeat Waylon Jennings:

> And it echoed through the canyon
> like the disappearin' dream
> of yesterday.

There is other music too. Perhaps we can be quieter now and then, and listen.

DAVID R. BROWER
President, Friends of the Earth

Berkeley, California
August 17, 1973

Jessie

ONE AFTERNOON during my first visit to Rose Yellowhair, her cousin, Jessie Whitesheep, came to see us. That was three years ago, a day that began a friendship with Jessie that took me back to the Reservation many times. Once I brought my eleven-year-old daughter Lindsey to meet Jessie in winter, and a two-day horizontal blizzard immobilized us for almost a week. The mud that followed the snow was as thick and impassable as the drifts. Once I brought my ten-year-old, Sally, and we spent a month in the relentless sun of July that brings the white haze of summer to the desert.

Jessie, through those years, helped me understand and pull into this century a line from a Navajo poem I read long before I met her: *The strength of the earth is my strength.*

Jessie guided me, as far as I was to be guided, through the intricacies of a very different human world. She would be uncomfortable if she believed I were representing her as the embodiment of the Navajos, or if I called upon her to speak for her people. She warned me once in her own way not to let a single person or incident carry me too far: We were having dinner in the Whitesheep hogan. My daughter Sally was eating the middle of her Oreos before she started her mutton stew. Jessie leaned over to her and whispered, "When I write a book about little Anglo girls I am going to say that they all eat their cookies before they eat their dinner."

Jessie is just Jessie, a young Navajo woman in her early twenties. She is fairly fluent in English. Often when we talked I sensed her frustration as she searched for words to tell what she was feeling. More often she used long silences and one-word answers. As I came to know her I asked questions. Mostly she did not answer, either because she did not understand or did not know, or sometimes because she did not want me to know, at least, not then. I understood her unspoken feeling that if I ought to know, I would find out—eventually, when the time was right. Jessie is not a public Navajo. Like most people in her community at Rough Rock in northeastern Arizona, she is a provincial person. Her cares, by and large, concern her daily existence. She lives with her parents, who speak only Navajo, and with a constellation of other relatives and her infant daughter, Lolita. Jessie does not know if she is going to marry Lolita's father or not. Perhaps some day, but for now he lives far away, too far away from her home.

To me Jessie is beautiful, but Jessie herself is shy and self-conscious about a roll of baby-fat around her middle. Once when a friend teased her about it she was quiet, then she quoted her mother: "If you don't nurse your baby you stay thin, but so does the baby. This way we're both fat!" Her friend laughed with her. She has not nursed her baby in more than a year.

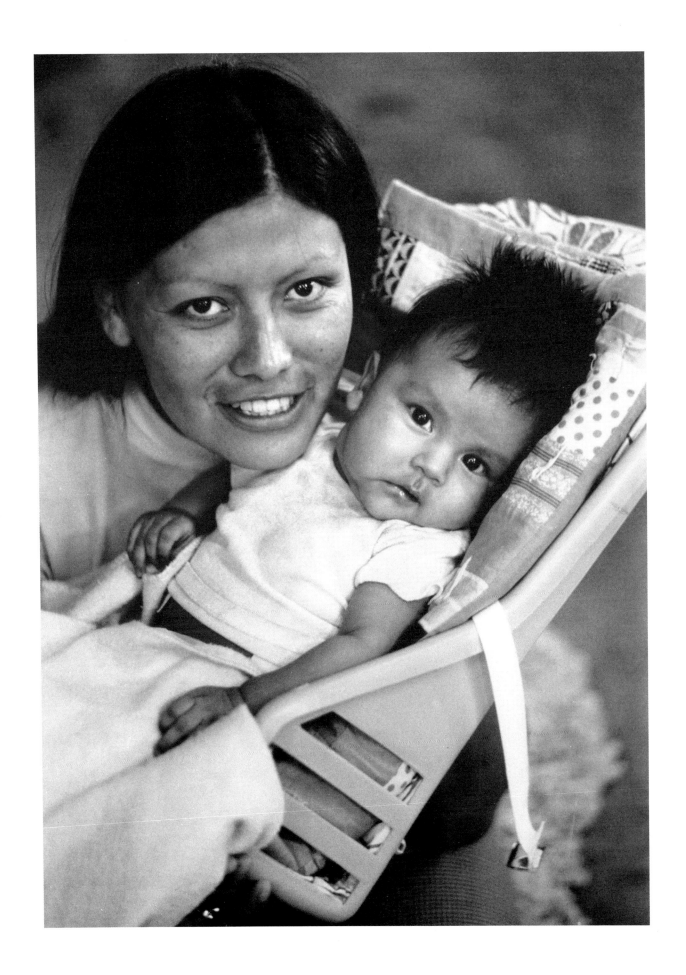

Jessie drives a new black-and-white pickup truck, slowly, because where she lives gasoline is very expensive. Except for the trading post, where they charge fifty-five cents a gallon, the nearest gas station is a sixty-mile round trip over a jaw-rattling dirt road full of potholes and patches of clay that, when wet, send you sliding off into the ditch. Gasoline is fifteen cents a gallon cheaper there, and Jessie would rather drive to the gas station than deal with the Anglo at the trading post anyway.

Jessie works as a primary school teacher's aide at the Rough Rock Demonstration School, a Navajo school for local children. She has a curious set of prized possessions: besides her pickup, she owns a battery-operated tape recorder, a baby goat, two big goats, and one sheep. She longs for more sheep.

Timeless, wind-worn rocks, a limitless sky, a horizon that ends the sky a hundred miles from her home, a silhouetted pinyon in the peach-colored dawn, the cries of a newborn lamb, long walks at dusk to gather the sheep after a day of work, endless sitting and spinning wool late into the night, long distances between small towns—all these slow the pace of life, and there is a gentle rhythm in the quiet of Jessie's world.

Camp and Family

EXCEPT for a few who hold jobs in Gallup, Shiprock, Page, or Kayenta, most Navajos do not live in villages or towns. Each family lives by itself, usually several generations together, in the middle of its grazing land in permanent camps. The Whitesheep camp is a scattering of three one-room houses, two hogans, one summer shade house made of cedar limbs and sheets of scrap plywood, two doorless outhouses with a view that stretches to the year-round snow-capped Sleeping Ute Mountain, to a sheep corral, and to a large and in its way quite beautiful pile of gnarled, sunbleached pinyon and cedar branches. The branches will fuel the fire in the sawed-in-half oil drum that serves as a heater in the winter, light source at nighttime, and stove all year round.

The camp is clustered beneath a sand- and boulder-strewn hill that is covered with rabbitbrush, sage, pinyons, wild onions, and a lacework of hundreds of sheep trails. Shards of pottery can still be found in the dry creek beds that wind down from Black Mountain, where two thousand years ago the Anasazi, "The Ancient Ones," had their pueblos.

Up close, within the cluster of buildings, the complex bustle of a large family camp is reassuring. From a distance, viewed from the roads on which tourists whip past, at a safe, antiseptic distance, Navajo camps seem forlorn, scanty settlements huddled tight against the earth. But even in the distance the dot of a family group, tiny against a vast earth and sky, sometimes seems magnificent. I saw such a camp once through new eyes—my daughter Lindsey's. At dawn, on her first visit to the Reservation, we were driving along the dirt road that leads from Many Farms to the Rough Rock Trading Post. The sun had just burned through the haze on the ash-blue horizon behind us. Black Mountain loomed ahead. As we drove, the world around us glowed a warm, pale salmon. The foothills rolled ahead thirty or forty miles to the mountain. The sky had grown the palest blue when suddenly there were tiny dancing flashes far to the northwest of us. I stopped the Volkswagen and asked Lindsey to figure out what the flashes were. She squinted, searching, and finally cried, "It's a house! It's the sun reflecting off the windows of a house. No, it's two or three houses." Before the reflection she had not seen them, those specks that melted into the distant yellow-orange boulders. It was Jessie's camp.

Rachel Whitesheep, Jessie's mother, owns the land. It once belonged to Rachel's mother. And before that, to Jessie's great grandmother. Rachel Whitesheep's family is from Dennehotso, thirty miles to the northeast. Bits of their land are strung out from there to the base of Black Mountain. When Jessie's father, who was from the top of the Mountain, married the girl who had been chosen for him by his parents, and whom he had never met, he followed Navajo custom and came to live on his wife's land. They picked a spot near the base of the mountain and built a hogan. It is gently rolling land on which, Jessie's mother remembers, the grass was high when she was first married. Now, some four decades later, the land has been overgrazed by the Whitesheep's increasing flock of sheep and goats.

When Jessie speaks English, plurals are misplaced and verbs stray from their usual places.

"This land is very important to us. We want to have enough for the livestocks to eat. The Navajo people really do care about land. It seems that people cares more for the land than anything else—because of their livestocks. People thinks that if they have more calves, more sheep, more this and that, it is like being wealthy. That's what it means to them. It means they're the richest family."

The "riches" of livestock are won from stubborn soil and mean climate. In the course of one of my cold winter visits the sky and air became a wet, hazy gray. Jessie wore her cyclamen-colored parka, vivid against the brooding sky and monochrome umbers and tans of the sheep close. Snow began to fall. It blew in circles and twisted upward, dark against the sky and very white against the mountain. At first the flakes were large and floated, almost dancing, flirting with the wind, changing moment by moment. Then the snow thickened and stuck to the backs of the sheep.

It snowed on and off for several days. The stock had started their birthing too early. When Jessie brought the animals in earlier in the week, she found twin goats frozen in the snow not far from the camp. So, although it was daytime when they usually wandered and foraged, today Mrs. Whitesheep was keeping the animals corraled so she could sort out the pregnant ones. According to Jessie, her mother and older sister have a way of knowing when a ewe is ready to give birth, but neither Jessie nor her father can tell.

When we went back to the warm hogan, a goat had just delivered on the hard, packed-earth floor. There were clots on the floor and the cord trailed the ground, as the kid tentatively stood up, its hair was covered with a thick substance the mother was trying to lick off. Both were close to the stove in the middle of the room. Lolita was much more interested in trying to crawl to the baby goat than she was in eating her fry-bread lunch.

Jessie's entire family was living in the hogan because they were still repairing the house where her parents usually sleep. The hogan is a windowless, eight-sided cedar log-and-earth one-room shelter with a ceiling that slants up to a central smoke hole. No part of the room is more than ten or twelve feet from the stove. Six adults, often more when other members of the family visit, and five children live and sleep in it. Boxes of cornflakes, canned baby formula, twenty-pound bags of flour, two-pound cans of tinned fruit and coffee, and a rusty alarm clock were stored in a large cupboard. Sheepskins, blankets, mattresses, and bedrolls were stacked against walls draped with brightly printed fabrics sent by Danny, one of the Whitesheep sons who worked in a cloth-printing factory in San Francisco before he returned to the Reservation. Tables lined one wall. They were piled with kerosene lamps, Coleman lanterns, and buckets filled with drinking water hauled in from a well some distance from the camp. Boxes and sacks were stuffed in the crevices and under the eaves. The family's clothes and laundry were stacked on the floor in large plastic bags; jackets and shirts hung on one of the lines alongside drying diapers. Lolita wears Pampers but her two-year-old cousin is allergic to them and wears cheesecloth diapers. Jessie says she would rather live in a hogan summer and winter than in a house. In the summer a hogan is cool, and in the winter it is easy to heat. Someday, though, she would like to have her own hogan.

Jessie's mother has a delicate, fine-featured face and a realist's intelligent eyes that often warm with humor. Her hair is gathered in an oblong roll and tied up with homespun yarn at the nape of her neck. She has a few wisps of gray at her temples. I am not sure how tall she is, for when I see her she is almost always sitting, whether to weave, cook, spin, or patiently squeeze out the intestine of a freshly butchered sheep. She appears to be a short, stout woman. She usually wears a traditional Navajo cotton or velvet blouse and fluted satin skirt, always in rich cranberry, cornflower, or woodviolet colors. I have never looked in her face for long because she is shy and my gaze makes her uncomfortable. I have never asked to photograph her, but on one visit she asked me to take a picture of her, a profile. I gave her a copy of the picture on my next visit, and she quickly put it away without a word. I wondered what she was thinking. Later I noticed that when visitors came to the hogan, she leaned over and took the picture from a stack of papers under a nearby table and, without smiling, showed it to them. Jessie told me that meant she liked the picture very much. I had been afraid that like many traditional Navajos she would have great difficulty with being photographed. She was brought up to believe that if her image were put on film her soul would become less than whole; when she died, a certain part of her would never be at rest.

I had already photographed John Whitesheep, Jessie's father. Years earlier, before I met Jessie, I had stopped my car to photograph the silhouette of a man on horseback bringing the sheep in for the evening, sun low behind them, dust blowing. Moments later the man wheeled his horse and came toward me at a gallop and, pulling alongside my window, stopped the horse, leaned down and said, "Two dollars, you take pictures." I paid him, thanked him, and was embarrassed. Next time I saw him, Jessie was introducing me to her father. He gave no sign that he remembered.

John Whitesheep is short and fair, with a slender nose and medium-thick glasses. He has a thick chest and belly and thin legs. Like many Navajo men, he never seems to take off his ten-gallon hat, indoors or out. He loves to tease. Gradually I came to realize that he is a tough man, inured to physical suffering and the vagaries of a rough climate. Once his thumb was gouged by a steer's horn, and the expression on his face never changed. He had Jessie drive him to the missionary house next to the trading post, where he could have his thumb stitched and bandaged. No matter what the temperature, John Whitesheep wears a plaid flannel shirt. Jessie told me he has a winter jacket, but I never saw him wear it. Years ago Mr. Whitesheep was a medicine man, and

recently he received a National Institute of Mental Health fellowship to relearn the Red Ant Way ceremony.

The Whitesheeps have ten children, seven girls and three boys, and twenty-eight grandchildren. Jessie is the next to youngest of her parents' children. Two other daughters and one son have returned to live in or near the family camp. Katherine Williams, the oldest daughter, is divorced and lives in the camp with her two children, Freddie and Martha. She is in her mid-forties and helps with the sheep and cooking. Like her mother, she wears traditional clothes and speaks only Navajo. Jessie's brother Peter and his wife and baby live there too. Jessie's sister, Liz Honie, works and lives at the nearby Rough Rock School with her husband and their four children. They have one of the few apartments in the boys' dormitory and have become the family's link with modern conveniences. They have running water, a washing machine, a shower where Jessie can wash her hair, a television set, and a telephone. The two-year-old daughter of another of Jessie's sisters lives at the camp. Both her parents work at the power plant at Page, but they prefer that their child be brought up in the closeness of the family. Jessie thinks they will work for awhile, get enough money to buy a pickup, and then come back closer to home. Alice, Jessie's teenage youngest sister, has been

blind since birth but nevertheless goes to school in Tucson. On school holidays she makes the arduous all-day trip home on public buses, transferring four times. When she returns to the camp she immediately takes up the job of babysitter.

When a Navajo baby first laughs out loud, the person who makes him laugh must give an enormous party. Everyone in the family comes and is fed. A ceremony is held called the Laughing Ceremony, in which the mother takes her baby's hand and sprinkles salt into the hand of everyone there, one by one. Each person chants a little prayer for the baby in hopes that he will not grow up to be stingy. The baby acknowledges them through his mother.

One winter when Jessie had finished her long teaching day, we sat inside the hogan and talked. Although the fire heated the hogan more than enough, Jessie never took off her bright pink jacket. Outdoors, even in the snow, she wore tennis shoes or flat-heeled leather dress shoes with her printed jeans or slacks. She thought my high-topped walking shoes were the funniest things she had ever seen and said she would rather be miserably cold going after the sheep than wear such clumping shoes. She called them my "dancing slippers" and told me that the old people were always laughing at them. Once I tried herding with Jessie in my sandals and returned with my toes painfully full of cactus spines. Jessie laughed. She was not sympathetic. "When I was a little girl I used to herd the sheeps barefoot. You just put your foot down in the sand and shove it forward a little way then you step down on it. That way you never get stuck." But it didn't work when I tried it.

I asked Jessie about the old people.

"Well, they've lived through a lot and they know what life is like, so we have to get advices from them. The young generations thinks that all the old people are like Ph.D.s. People say that old people are important; they know what is right and what is wrong. Probably some young people say they don't care now, but I think they do. The way I see it, it seems that everbody has respect for older people. Like my parents, they always tell me not to make fun of old men and ladies, how they dress and how they talk, 'cause we are all going to go through that too. Old people tell us what we are doing wrong and that we shouldn't just be loafing around. They tell us to find a job, not to sit around with our hands crossed on our lap. When a Navajo couple is married they do not promise each other a thing. Instead, they invite all the old people from their clans and the community. The old people take turns telling the couple about marriage, the hardships, temptations and responsibilities. They have known the couple since they were born. Sometimes it gets really embarrassing, hearing about all the things you did wrong when you were younger. They tell us to work."

"Do they tell you to go make a lot of money?"

"No, that doesn't matter. They tell us not to be stingy."

She gave me an example of Navajo generosity:

"If someone you don't even know comes to your house you have to cook for them, feed them, you know, things like that. You can't just sit back and say you don't care who he is. Like we had about four ladies who came up from Rock Point. We had never even heard of them before, but they were looking for a certain plant and they heard that my dad knew where it grew. My mom started cooking right away as soon as she saw them. They were really thankful and after we ate, my dad took them up to the mountain to help them find the plant. Then they gave us back something because we helped them. That's the way we do it."

The story made me sad about our own peculiar attitude toward gifts. Many Anglos feel put upon when Navajos seem to expect food or money after a visit. Jessie explained the Navajo concept of exchanging when we first started visiting her friends; she asked me to bring along gifts of coffee, oranges, flour, and cookies.

Gingerly, I asked Jessie about the old peoples' feeling about legends. For a long time she sat staring at the ground. Finally she said, "I can't talk to you about

those things." There was more silence, and I was afraid that I had offended her. I remembered hearing that legends could only be told in the winter, but it *was* winter. We had eight inches of snow the night before. When I tried to make this point, she said, "It is not winter now. We have passed the fourth full moon. That was back in February."

Suddenly she saw that as funny and she laughed. Different clans, she explained, believe winter ends at different times. Some believe that the first rain signals spring; others that winter ends when the first snake comes out. Jessie's clan believes it comes with the fourth moon. She would ask her father about counting the moons, and where the cycle starts—next winter.

Like her mother, Jessie likes to weave, but she told me once, "It is too much, you know. You have to start carding, then tending the wool and dyeing it and all of that. You have to go spinning and you have to make real different colors. Then you have to make your loom and then you start doing your weaving. It takes quite a while to set up a loom. My mom, it seems like she has in her head what she is going to do. It is like a silversmith. He always knows how he is going to make a design. My mom, she never says she is going to do it this way or that way. She just starts off. Some of her designs her mom taught her, and some she does because it is a way she wants to express herself."

Mrs. Whitesheep is one of the most respected Navajo weavers, Jessie told me: "She sold her rug at the trading post for $400. They even put her rug in a book. One rug she made had a blue ribbon at the Phoenix Fair, and they wanted to know who she was so they could pay her more. But my mom didn't get a chance to go all the way to Phoenix."

Jessie did not know the name of the book her mother's rug was in. She saw the book at the high school, but the students had lost the cover. She did not expect to see the book again.

"They had my dad's name and they said his wife did the weaving. I guess they didn't know her name."

When I asked her about male and female roles around the house she told me that you often see women tagging along behind their husbands when they are walking "together" or you see them huddled in the back of a pickup while the men ride up front. But women have a high status within the family; the fact that couples usually live with the wife's people is one indication. Another is that the most important and powerful Holy

People are female. Children are born into their mother's clan and a woman can always weave a rug and make extra income. There is no joint property among Navajos. Whoever owns a pickup drives it. Girls play basketball and have teams of their own. They own horses and ride them and compete in the rodeo barrel races.

As the early-spring sun began warming the land and drying the mud, Jessie and I walked to some of her favorite places. We searched for plants that Mrs. Rachel Whitesheep uses for dyes and that she collects all year long, whenever their season is right. She keeps them in the one-room storehouse in their camp, along with forty or so extra sheepskins, large dusty bags of wool to be spun, grain for the sheep and the surplus of government-issue cans of peaches, pears, and other staples.

The sheep have grazed most of the land near the hogan too closely, so that to find dye plants we had to go closer to the mountain. Jessie pointed out a bitterball that blooms in early summer:

"People say that plant makes a greenish dye but my mom won't use it. It is a special plant used in the ceremonies. I never pick that plant. My dad always tells me not to fool around with plants. Some of them make you go blind if you touch them. If you touch another plant that you are not supposed to touch you can swell up."

"What if you are walking and your foot touches it accidentally?"

"That's okay. You just got to not touch it with your hand. There are many plants I don't really know about so I don't bother them. Insects, too. Someone in Lee Caboni's family got a red ant bite. Now the whole family has kidney problems, bad ones. His sister is on the kidney machine. Lee couldn't ride a horse for a year and he couldn't control his bowels, too. He will have to have a ceremony."

Jessie pointed to a beeplant, which would be covered with lavender blossoms in late summer:

"But this plant is okay. During the bad times people ate it and it saved them from starving, my dad said. My grandmother still makes spinach out of it.

"My mom takes this plant before the flowers come. She mashes up lots and lots of leaves, about a bushel, and takes out the stalks. Then she boils it in a gallon of water. She leaves the yarn in for one week and boils it for one hour again, then lets it sit for another week. It makes a yellowish green."

Yellows seem to be the easiest colors to make. The shade can be controlled by varying the time the wool is soaked or by changing the type of pot in which it is cooked. Jessie showed me Owl's Claw, a yellow daisy. Her mother picks the fresh blossoms and boils them in an enamel pot for several hours. After the wool soaks overnight, it becomes a vivid yellow. If she boils them half the time and doesn't soak the wool overnight, it becomes a pale yellow. If she uses an aluminum pot, she gets a mustard color. The Whitesheeps gather orange rock lichens after summer rains to make an orange dye and they use the thick, brick-colored rainwater that collects in puddles in a sandstone canyon near Chilchinbito, halfway between Rough Rock and Dennehotso, to make a salmon pink.

In season Jessie picks the fruit of the prickly pear and rubs it in the sand with her foot to remove the spines. Then her mother mashes the fruit, strains it, and covers the yarn with water and the cactus mash. She checks the fermenting liquid many times a day for a week or so, each time rubbing dye into the yarn until she has a warm rose color.

I had seen Mrs. Whitesheep's rugs before I met Jessie and had been excited by their powerful geometric designs made with warm earth-colored dyes. Younger women seem to use more gayly colored dyes. Mrs. Whitesheep makes a soft, brownish red dye of her own by boiling rootbark from mountain mahogany. Jessie says her mother mixes rootbark with other plants to get a rosier red or pinker tan, but she doesn't know the English name for the other plants.

Out of shyness and politeness Mrs. Whitesheep keeps her face turned from me and never looks in my eyes. She rarely speaks, although she did many kind things for my children and me. On one trip I took some of my niece's too-small clothes to Lolita. Mrs. Whitesheep was sitting on a rug in the hogan. She took the clothes and just sat without saying a word. She turned her back to me. I sat talking to my daughter, Lindsey, wondering if I should leave or wait for Mrs. Whitesheep to indicate what she wanted me to do. I could not tell whether she was pleased or insulted. A long fifteen minutes later she turned to us and held up Lolita, who had been playing on the floor nearby. She had dressed her in the frilliest pink pinafore and had made three tufts of braid on top of her head, and had perched a white lace pokebonnet behind them. Lolita had had her face and dribbly nose scrubbed and Mrs. Whitesheep was beaming. She offered us some pinto beans and coffee.

The Navajos I have met don't say "thank you" or "please" spontaneously, as Anglos do—or even at all. That afternoon, as members of the family came in they shook our hands lightly, then began speaking softly to Mrs. Whitesheep. Jessie's brother, Peter, finally looked over at me.

"We do not say 'thank you' the way you do," he said, "but you might not understand what we feel, so I will say it to you. We do not say, 'I am sorry,' either. If something bad happens to a family we go and stay with them as many days as we are needed, but we never mention what is sad or wrong. We just stay and help and they know what we feel, I guess."

When we left for home after that visit, Mrs. White-

sheep gave me some wool she had sheared and spun, so I could knit a sweater for my husband, and she butchered a sheep for our dinner. I helped, and Jessie told me about butchering.

"When we butcher a sheep we sing a little song for him. In the old days the hunter sang to the deer that he knew the deer's life was as precious as his, but he must kill, so his children could have food to eat. He explained that the deer's life would continue in his body and he said not to worry. We have a song like that for the sheep.

"I don't know why, but we always get a piece of wool and put it in his mouth. Sometimes he spits it out, but that's okay. We are not supposed to grab the wool before we butcher him or the mutton will get bruised. And we are not supposed to get hold of his horn—that is bad luck. We tie his hands and feet crossed, all four together, so each foot is going in a different direction and he doesn't wiggle. We cut his neck with a knife and put the blood in a pan. Then we cook the blood with potatoes, corn, salt, and chili peppers. We wash out the stomach and put the stuffing in. It is sort of like a tamale after we have sewn it up with a piece of sharp wood and boiled it for an hour or so."

Sheep are the lifeblood of the Navajo family. Jessie's father told her that the people have songs and prayers for sheep and horses, but not for goats and cows. Jessie explained that as long as there were hungry people, they would never slaughter a sheep and insult him by throwing out his eyes, intestines, or stomach. Every part of him is eaten, and his skin is slept on as a mattress.

Freshly charcoaled mutton dinner was the perfect way to end a visit that I didn't want to end. Jessie stuffed the stomach, and Mrs. Whitesheep cut large lengthwise slices of ribs and cooked them outdoors over a grill held up by old coffee cans. The juices dripped on the glowing cedar logs, and quick blue flames danced for a few seconds, then disappeared into the red coals. Mrs. Whitesheep also made some kneeldown bread. She ground fresh corn and made a mush, which she wrapped in corn husks. She dug a hole, put in hot ashes, laid the corn across them and covered them with leaves and sand. She built her fire over that and when the mutton was ready, so was the bread.

While Jessie was cooking, her niece's black kitten kept trying to jump on the bench and drag a piece of mutton away. After a while, Jessie shouted for someone to put him outside. When Jessie is yelling instructions to someone in Navajo her voice is gutteral and abrupt. The kids glower, but mind her quickly.

Finally the dinner was cooked. We sat on old sheets and blankets spread on the floor. The Whitesheeps were out of Coleman fuel, so we used two kerosene lanterns for light. Even the little children filled their plates twice. Jessie's father had brought cottage cheese from the trading post, and for dessert we had it with canned peaches and a chocolate cake that Lindsey had baked that afternoon in one of the apartments at the Rough Rock School. Mr. Whitesheep spoke quietly and with a straight face, but Jessie giggled at everything he said. She translated for me, most of the time telling me it was useless to try because he was making puns in Navajo that were meaningless in English.

Navajo is a great language for puns. Most people love to tease, using puns to do the work. I was easy prey for Mr. Whitesheep, for often I had difficulty in distinguishing between a sound and a nonsound, as when a nasal almost-cluck in the back of the throat in the middle of a word alters its meaning. For example, *tsin* means log, stick, or tree, and *ts'in* means bone. A Whitesheep family joke about me was that the first time I met the family I mispronounced the Navajo word *ya ta hey*, which means "hello," by adding a barely audible sound as I finished the word, a sound made more by closing my mouth too soon than by uttering anything. By that slight mistake I had said to Mr. Whitesheep, "I am able to give birth to babies very easily." Jessie consoles me by saying that the mistake is a common one made by Anglos trying to speak the complicated Navajo language and that I amused her father greatly.

The language is difficult for an Anglo to learn for the additional reason that there are few similarities between Navajo and English patterns of grammar and thought. A Navajo thinks of himself as neither more nor less than any other force of nature, and his language reflects this. He would not say, "I have a headache." Instead he would say, "A pain is hurting my head."

"Some of the words are old-fashioned types," Jessie says, "and you don't have anything to say when you translate them. You have to use another word or example. Old people have a habit of using old-fashioned words that you don't hear every day. When we interpret we have to find a new word for whites to understand. And the young generation has slang Navajo. Some of the older people complain about that."

After dinner John Whitesheep saddled his horse and rode out to round up the other horses and herd them to the well several miles away. Then he herded the horses back to the camp, where he penned them for the night. By nightfall the desert was clear and dark. With no electric lights to compete with the stars, the sky seemed enormous and I felt quite small. In the distance there was the lonely barking of a dog. Occasionally a sheep bleated. The wind rustled the pinyons, and I felt the familiar sadness of having to leave.

Rains

IT WAS late summer and there had been neither rain nor snow for nine months. The desert was hot and gray and parched. Long cracks split the earth, and all the shrubs and trees were covered by sand and dull dirt. During the daytime there was a harsh glare. Then, toward dusk, the sky would fill with black thunderheads and a hot wind would rush across the land, whipping the sand into a frenzy, matting it in the tangled wool of the sheep and driving it under the doors and windows of the hogans in its path. Lightning forked wildly from the clouds, and the echo of the thunder was as frightening as the fury of the skies. But then, after all this preparation, only a few drops of rain would fall to a brittle, thirsty desert.

The President of the United States declared the Rough Rock Community a disaster area.

My daughter Sally and I went to spend a month at the Whitesheep camp. Jessie, her nine-year-old niece Martha, and Sally and I were herding sheep the evening the rains came. At first a few warm drops fell and sent the arid smell of hot dust tingling in the back of our noses. Then the clouds opened and a chilling rain beat on us, lashing hard across the desert. Tumbleweeds, wet and muddy, blew against our legs and then off beyond us where they tangled among the herd. Breaking free of the animals, they continued their reckless journey, bouncing off a rock here, a pinyon there, until they were gone. We stood with our backs hunched to the wind, shivering, thankful for the rains but frightened of the lightning. Soon the rains blew by and the clouds scattered. The

storm had coaxed a poignant sweet smell from the sagebrush, the earth smelled moist and fresh, and the plants had been washed clean of their accumulation of dust. We saw delicate silver greens, lemon greens, pale chartreuse greens, and blue greens.

We moved on. The sheep bells clinked a counterpoint to the soft talk among a family of Gambrel quail. Nighthawks left their daytime roosts in the pinyons and swooped and glided away from the fading sun, going after sphinx moths or click beetles. The spiritual home of the Navajos, the monoliths of Monument Valley, were faint mauve silhouettes far away to the north that evening, as the clouds blew over and the dusk darkened and became evening. Sky was everywhere and the desert became still. For me it was an extraordinarily sensuous night.

For Jessie it had always been this way.

During the next week the sky stayed dark with rain. Runoffs dug new arroyos in the land and the roads were impassable because of flash floods that raced down the washes. Large pools of water stood in the sand and spread across the road. Pickups had to drive around them, over the rabbitbrush. The pools filled miraculously with countless frogs, chirruping and singing. Many believe, Jessie told me, that the rain turns into frogs when it hits the ground. Jessie loves the nighttime, when the frogs' plaintive calls go on long after the other animals are silent. She has never learned where the frogs go during the long droughts.

Plants

WHEN THE skies cleared, Jessie resumed teaching me about plants. She led me across the desert, the sun hot on our backs and the sky a deep blue before us.

"Let's dig up this yucca," she said. "I crush the roots and wash my hair with them. It always gives me a little rash, but that goes away in a few hours. I don't think all those chemicals in blue and green shampoos can ever go away."

We were visiting Mildred James and her husband Big Legs. The James' camp was on a high bouldery ridge overlooking a red sandstone canyon near Chilchinbito. There were no trees, just a low scattering of large yucca; it was a bleak, lunar landscape. Mildred was sitting on a mattress outside the summer shade house when we came up, and Big Legs stood shyly in the shade by the side of his house. When we had talked for awhile Mildred began teasing me because I have three daughters and no sons.

"You can pay Big Legs money to have boys," she said. "His own boys tease him about his knowledge of herbs. He denies it, but I brag about him to everyone." Mildred could brag in fluent English, Navajo, Spanish or French.

When we left I asked Jessie if there was an herb that could determine a child's sex and she nodded.

"It's a special plant. Just certain ones know which one. Some medicine men do, some not, and some old people know who learned it from their clans. There has to be a prayer that goes along with the plant. My cousin had boys all the way— six boys—and she wanted a little girl and then they had to use that plant. I don't know the name in English. I haven't even seen one yet; it is not common. Just the ones that knows the plant, they are the only ones that knows what to do and what it looks like. We don't even know. Marlene Grayeyes couldn't have a baby at all so Big Legs James made a special plant for her and now she has one. And there is another plant that you can use if you want to have lots of kids."

"Would it work on someone who was not a Navajo?"

"I don't know, maybe."

The large yucca leaves are used in the peyote ceremony, so Jessie does not touch them. The middle part of the yucca plant has been useful to the Whitesheep family. Last summer, some of the family's sheep went blind. Jessie believes it was because of something in the Grazing Committee's sheep dip. (The Navajo Tribe has a Grazing Committee that oversees each area's annual livestock branding, innoculating, and dipping.) John Whitesheep's mother told him that if he burned the stalk of the yucca—slicing it thin and putting it in a pan and heating it until it crumbled—and then mixed the ashes with iodine, he would be able to cure each blind sheep by putting the mixture in its eyes. John tried it, and the cure worked.

Black Mountain

WHENEVER there was time I asked Jessie to take me up to the top of the mountain where many of her family still live, where the air is cool, and where there are long-stretching wildflower meadows and forests of yellow pine, juniper and gambel oak. Sometimes during my visits I became very depressed that I was a photographer, that I walked with mechanical inventions of the twentieth century slung across my shoulder in a camera bag, and that I flew casually, and when *I* wished, in and out of the lives of people I was fond of. I think most of the people of the community had come to know me. Some had become friends and might even look forward to my next visit, hoping I would bring them pictures from the last. Some might wonder which daughter I would bring this time. Some might be afraid I would want to photograph them when they didn't want me to. I always carried two cameras, although Jessie's cousin, Priscilla Begay, told me to carry just one, hide it, and then sneak pictures because her people don't like to be photographed. I couldn't do that. If I were going to photograph a family, I would try to stay with them several days—helping haul water, herd sheep, and chop wood, trying to learn a few words of Navajo, always wearing the cameras but not using them. Then I would let the children take pictures. Finally I would begin photographing. Then it became fun, and we played and clowned for pictures. At last, I think the cameras went unnoticed, and that's when the photographing really began.

To persuade shy people to trust you can cause strain, and occasionally I wondered why I was there, whether everyone would not be better off if nothing came from the outside world to foul things up—me, the Peabody Coal Mine, the Bureau of Indian Affairs, or the missionaries. Those were the times I would try to persuade Jessie to take me to the cool seclusion of Black Mesa.

The road to the mountain runs west from the White-sheep's. It winds and twists, climbing into the foothills through rock and scrub pines, its scar usually invisible from a distance. Trails lead off toward unseen family camps, and it is difficult to tell which are the family tracks and which is the main road. The edge of the mesa looms fifteen hundred feet above, dark with foliage.

The long road up the rocky wall is two deep ruts a pickup's width apart, with a shoulder little more than a foot wide. In three or four places there are laybys, should one pickup meet another. Mudslides and falling rocks have scarred the tracks so that we always drove at a crawl. The road cuts back and forth across the rock, zigzagging steeply upward. There is nothing to prevent a pickup from slipping off the side, although none ever has, as far as anyone can remember. During the last winter the two front wheels of Wade Honie's truck did slip off the edge. His wife Linda leapt from the passenger side and hung on to the slats on the bed of the truck until Wade could climb out, get a rope, wind it around a boulder and a tree and tie it to one of the back wheels. The front of the truck hung out over an eight-hundred-foot drop. The Honies walked several miles to the nearest camp and got help to pull the truck back onto the narrow road.

As Jessie and I drove up, we could see in the distance the Lukachukai Mountains in New Mexico, splashes of snow on a lower range of the Rockies in Colorado, and Monument Valley in Utah. Around us hundreds of square miles of the Navajo Nation were spread out like a counterpane. The shadows of clouds blew across the land, changing its colors.

On the face of one of the rocks was a faded hand-painted sign saying "Welcome to Black Mesa" and beside it a fresher, spray-can painted peace symbol and the words "make love not war." When she saw the newer sign, Jessie laughed and said that one of the Grayeyes boys must have made it, probably Eugene.

I remembered meeting Eugene once. He stalked over to me as I was standing by the trading post and said, "You have to pay me two thousand dollars if you want to take my picture." Knowing that Navajos love teasing, I replied, "No, you have it all wrong, I am a very famous photographer and you must pay *me* two thousand dollars to take *your* picture!"

Eugene studied me solemnly.

"I've seen you up on the mountain," he said, "I know who you are. Do you know who I am? I am Eugene Somebody-Anybody-Nobody-Everybody. I live on the mountain."

He tipped his cowboy hat, smiled for the first time, and walked away.

As we drove on the road wound in and out across the wildflower meadows and dry arroyos. Bluetailed lizards skittered in and out among the rocks. A red-tailed hawk that had been slowly circling overhead dropped suddenly toward a chipmunk that was sunning on one of the rocks, indifferent, it seemed, too seemingly lazy and unconcerned about the world around him. In an instant the chipmunk's tail shot into the air and he jumped sideways so quickly that he seemed to somersault as he dove into the black crevice behind him, safe from the hawk.

As she drove, Jessie told me about the importance of Black Mountain to her family during the defeat of the Navajos in the nineteenth century. During the summer of 1863, she said, Navajos were told to surrender unconditionally to the United States Army at Fort Defiance, Arizona. Those who did not would be considered hostile and captured or killed. None surrendered. Colonel Kit Carson led a troop of cavalry and laid waste a Navajo Nation that until then had been lush, and would never be so again.

In the course of the next two months the cavalry destroyed every corn, bean and pumpkin patch, cut down every fruit tree, slaughtered and left to rot hundreds of thousands of sheep, burned every hogan, and killed any Navajos who got in the way. By autumn most of the Navajo herds and grain had been destroyed, and many of the Navajos had hidden in the depths of Canyon de

Chelly. Jessie's great-grandmother was about eight years old and hid there with her younger brother and their parents. Jessie's great granduncle, Big Man's Brother, fled from the cavalry to Black Mountain. Carson's men, after destroying more than 5,000 peach trees and all the sheep in the Canyon, set up a blockade at the entrance and waited until winter came. Many Navajos froze to death. Others, unable to reach the yucca fruit or beeplant growing in the canyon, starved to death. In eleven days Colonel Carson and his men rounded up the rest and started them toward Fort Wingate. That was in January. Throughout the rest of the winter and into March, amid severe snowstorms, about eight thousand Navajos straggled into the Fort and were moved to Bosque Redondo at Fort Sumner, 350 miles to the southeast. On that "Long Walk" as it is called by the Navajos, many of the people were naked and froze to death. Those who were too sick to walk were shot. Finally, after four years, the survivors signed a treaty and were allowed to return to their land.

Jessie's great-grandmother and her family joined Big Man's Brother on Black Mountain and began to rebuild their lives. His nephew, John Hadley, was her grandfather and a respected medicine man on the reservation. On my first visits I was unsure whether John Hadley's cool eyes and tight smile meant shyness or contempt for an Anglo visitor—until I photographed him with his infant grandson, and for an instant he unbent.

One time we met John Hadley's fourteen-year-old son, Teddy, who had been kept from schools all his life and was being trained by his father to become a medicine man, a great honor for a boy. Teddy wore his hair in the traditional style, long and tied in a knot low on the back of his neck. He wore a black wide-brimmed hat like those I had seen old medicine men wear and he spoke only Navajo. But there all tradition ended. He lived with his blue Honda. He herded sheep with it, racing and jumping little hills, disappearing over the folds of the mesa. He also went for rides on his own when he was not working, wandering lazily into the deep purple shadows of the mountain washes, off in his own world.

During the nine-month drought of 1971-72, Navajos pleaded with John Hadley to hold a Rain Prayer, an ancient, complicated, and little-known ceremony. John Hadley is one of the few medicine men on the whole Reservation who can perform the five day ceremony. It must be done the old way. Men who attend must wear pants with buttons, not zippers. Food eaten during the five days must be hand ground and cooked in old pottery and iron. There can be no modern utensils or food. This is unlike many of the larger, more popular ceremonies, which often resemble carnivals, with canteen trucks selling popcorn, soft drinks, candy bars, and perhaps a bootlegger's truck backed in among the pickups on a no-liquor Reservation, and portable generators to power electric lights strung across the desert to light the dances.

Jessie did not attend the Rain Prayer because Lolita was sick, but her father did and she told me part of what he had told her about it. The first two days the medicine man came in and prepared an offering of jet, turquoise, abalone, and white shell. The third day he made a mixture of herbs, pollen, water, and 'medicine.' A boy and a girl sprinkled the mixture on each other, dancing clockwise in a carefully prescribed ritual, invoking par-ticular supernatural beings, using colors, directions, herbs, pollens, and prayers that symbolized the themes of harmony. They repeated this ritual four times, once for each of the great sacred mountains.

A Blessing Way Ceremony followed. The men went into a sweat house to purify themselves. After the shells were offered there were other prayers and the offering was taken to a remote place where the sheep would not be around it; it was hung on a tree that has been struck by lightning, hung so high it could not be seen. The Blessing, Jessie said, is for protection. It is held at the end of most healing ceremonies and is often sung by families at their hogans. There are a few songs one night, a ritual bath in yucca suds with prayers and songs the next day, and then singing that lasts through the night. There is much symbolism in it, and generous use of cornmeal, pollen, and pulverized blossoms.

Jessie is confident that her grandfather's ceremony brought the rain that deluged the desert with thunderstorms days later and set it wildly abloom with the moist, translucent yellow prickly pear cactus, flowering ash, and the sweet cliff rose, which Jessie and I could smell long before we could see it.

On the mountain Jessie and I stopped for lunch. We sat eating our sandwiches by an old windmill, feeling very relaxed in the warm afternoon breeze. The windmill creaked and hummed above us; the water sloshed below. The sky was a deep, clear blue, and a few fluffy clouds floated lazily along. A flock of prairie horned larks, not frightened by our being there, ran along the ground pecking weedseed. Their bright yellow faces ducked in and out of the budding yellow desert marigolds. Suddenly they flushed for no apparent reason, and flew into the air, high, high, almost out of sight. Then down they came, singing cheery, bubbly songs, floating, playing, and circling again toward the sky.

Ghosts

WE WERE talking quietly of Jessie's uncle, whose horses were watering at the trough below us. I happened to ask her what his mother's name was. Jessie pulled her shoulders up tight and shrugged the question off. I asked again, thinking I had spoken too rapidly and that she had not understood. She said merely, "She's gone," and there was a long silence. Finally she added: "She was a Christian. I guess it's okay," and she told me her name. Navajos do not like to speak the name of a person who has died. Death is horrible to them. Except for old people or the newborn dying a natural death, a person becomes a ghost after death. No matter how kind he was in his lifetime, in his death he becomes malevolent and returns to avenge any wrongdoing he suffered. Ghosts must be avoided; they cause sickness or death to those who encounter them. If a person dies inside a house, it is immediately abandoned and children must not play near it. On a visit long ago, I asked Jessie's cousin, Priscilla Begay, if she would take me to some Anasazi ruins which were near her camp on Black Mountain. She told me that I must never go there. I would get sick, because people had died there. I did not go.

Several years before I met Jessie, I had a bad experience on the Reservation. Remembering it bothered me every time I returned, and I decided now to talk to her about it.

She stared at the ground while I spoke, interrupting to question me only twice, and sat without speaking long after I finished the story.

It had been in the summer and I had come to the Reservation for a two-week visit to photograph the Navajo Tribal Ceremonial at Window Rock. Before the Ceremonial I went to Rough Rock to deliver a batch of pictures to Rose Yellowhair and her family. Two earlier packages had been lost in the mail and I heard the Yellowhairs were anxious to talk to me. As there seemed to be no way to get in touch with them, I called the school and asked if they could find me a place to stay while I tried to find the family on the mountain. A woman at the school assured me she would help. I arrived at night and she sent me to a house on the school grounds where one of the Anglo teachers lived. It was sparsely furnished with a few tables and chairs, a sofa, and a mattress on the bedroom floor. There were stacks of clothes scattered about on packing boxes for want of a bureau. The teacher, whose name was Frank, generously gave me his bedroom and slept in a sleeping bag on the sofa.

The next morning at breakfast I mentioned that on an earlier trip I had had dinner several times with a gentle, poetic Anglo, a photographer and teacher, who was being apprenticed in sacred medicine plants and herbs by an old medicine man. I said the young man had lived in one of the nearby houses and that I was anxious to see him again. Frank replied, "Oh, that was Martin. He used to live here. He's dead now. He committed suicide, right in that room"—my bedroom. I was saddened by the news of the death of a sensitive person I had liked very much. But a feeling of horror came too, because a house on the Reservation where a person had died was being lived in. Frank said that he didn't mind living there. Although he had a good rapport with his students, he felt no inclination to accept Navajo cultural beliefs, and was not, he said, superstitious. To me, the harmony in which the Navajos I had met seemed to live was inseparable from their belief in the supernatural and nourished by their religion. I was acutely

sensitive to this and found myself accepting Navajo beliefs and trying to live within them. I would certainly never ignore them while I was on the Reservation.

Depressed, I tried fitfully to find something to get my mind off Martin. I looked for friends, but all the Anglos I had met at the school were away for summer break. I thought I would drive, but the sand had drifted so high that my car wouldn't climb the first part of the road leading to the Yellowhair camp on the mountain. I tried concentrating on scenery, but smoke from one of New Mexico's most destructive fires, one that had destroyed several hundred thousand acres of trees in Carson National Forest, had drifted three hundred miles to the west; because of the haze, Black Mountain, a few miles beyond the school, was not visible. I tried walking to the trading post. It was a hot, parched, dusty day. I found Rose Yellowhair and several of her children there. I felt sudden relief. Using sign language I indicated to her that I had many pictures for her family and

that I would go get them. She pointed to me, to her pickup, to the mountain, raised her eyebrows to ask if I would come for the day. I nodded yes, and pointed to her and the truck and held up my hand to say "wait," and indicated that I would go get the pictures, which I had left at Frank's. I did not ask her to drive me because I had the feeling she wanted to stay and visit friends who had gathered at the trading post to socialize. She nodded and shyly pointed to the food counter, sweeping her hand back and forth. I agreed and asked the trader to box a case of Shasta Cola and some cookies and oranges.

I ran most of the mile and a half back to the compound, my feet slipping in the loose sand. I was excited at finding the Yellowhairs, a project I had thought would take me several days, but mostly I was thankful to be able to get up on the cool mountain where the grass was, where there were many watering places, and where I could see Charlene and some old familiar faces.

When I got to Frank's house it was locked. His pickup was gone. I ran to the school and searched the classrooms and offices for him. I rushed over to the cafeteria and the gym. He was nowhere. I dragged myself back to the house and began trying the windows. The windows in the back were high, about level with my eyes. The window by my bedroom was open about an inch and I wiggled it and pushed and got the bottom half open enough to crawl through. The problem was getting up high enough to squeeze through, and after a search of the yard had yielded no ladder or box on which to climb, I decided that I could put my hands on the sill, jump hard, keeping my head low, and get my head and shoulders through the opening and climb in. I made a strong leap, pulling up with my arms too hard, for I crashed into the metal rim of the window with the top of my head. I fell backward, unconscious. When I came to, I started vomiting. I reached for the top of my head. It had not been cut but there was a lump so large that when I put my palm against it my fingers could not reach down and touch the rest of my head. I don't know how long I lay there. I went around to the front of the house and sat on the step. I was dizzy and sick and hot and thirsty and tired.

Frank arrived soon afterward. I told him I would probably be on the mountain for a few days. He said he was going camping in Colorado for a week and gave me his key. I didn't know if I should leave and get a doctor in Gallup or if the cool air and Yellowhair children on the mountain would cheer me up and my head would take care of itself. In the end I went to the mountain to spend the day with the Yellowhairs.

Rose Yellowhair's fourteen-year-old daughter, Shirley, was home from school in Albuquerque. We talked as we herded the sheep. She was at an age where she wanted to discuss her many boy friends. When she grew up, she said, she wanted to marry a Hawaiian boy, because "they are so cute!" She wanted to get away from the Reservation and all the work she had to do around the camp. She thought she might be a nurse's aide, some day.

Shirley came down off the mountain with me. She was planning to stay with her cousin until the next day, when I had promised to drive them to the Ceremonial in Window Rock a hundred twenty miles away. She asked me where I was staying. I told her, reluctantly,

and she became intensely curious. Did I have any bad dreams? Did I sleep in the room where Martin died? Did I feel anything? Hear anything? Could she come in and use the shower to wash her hair?

"No," I said, and was very firm about that. I was worried by my head and didn't feel like talking about the matter anyway. But that night I heard a dull thump at Frank's door, then another, and finally I went to see what it was. Shirley Yellowhair and Linda Begay were standing there, each with a flashlight.

"We want to sleep here and see if anything happens," Shirley said.

They had walked from their cousin's camp several miles through the night. Most Navajos are afraid to be outside after dark, as most evil and ghostly activities take place then. But I said no again.

"We have no place to go," Shirley said. "We told our mothers we were coming here and they said it was all right."

That could not be true. I stuck to my no. They stood fast. After about fifteen minutes I realized that they were not going back to their camps, so I angrily loaded them into my car, packed my camera gear, and drove them to Window Rock. We arrived about one in the morning and I checked us into the Navajo-run Window Rock Motel.

As Jessie listened to the conclusion of my story, her face was tense. She said nothing.

"Does that make a difference in my life?" I asked.

There was a long silence. Jessie would not look at me and would not speak. Finally she said, "For you and me. I don't think it will bother me."

"Will there be bad spirits in me that could travel to you or Lolita when I am with you?"

First she said nothing. Then, "No."

"Is it dangerous for you to be with me?"

"No," she said slowly.

"Do you believe I will die or have an accident? Will what happened be bad luck for my health or my mind or my body?"

Jessie sat staring at the ground. Then she said, "Body or mind."

After a long silence she asked, "Was the woman who got you that house a Navajo?"

"No."

"Is she still living near here?"

"No."

"You will not die, but you probably will have an accident in the future."

I thought for a moment. "Does an Anglo have the same spirit as a Navajo?"

"I guess in a way he does."

Again there was a long silence, and she said, "Navajos say that you've got to believe in a certain thing for it to work for you. If you don't believe in anything then it's the same way. That's the way we understand."

"Do you have to believe in it for it to work against you? What if some Anglo went in the house and said, 'I don't believe it'; is it still bad for him?" I was thinking of Frank and his indifference to Navajo belief.

"It still is. 'Cause he's against it. Whether he cares or not, he is still against it."

It was a painful, choppy conversation. Sometimes Jessie's words did not make sense, but her feelings came through. For a while I was afraid that our friendship had suffered a severe blow. I avoided revealing that the teenagers were her cousins. They were just two girls from high school.

Commenting upon their curiosity, Jessie thought it was crazy.

"I mean, it seems that they are asking for it. If I was them I wouldn't even go near that house. I don't think it's right for you to go near that house now.

"Where did you sleep?"

I told her again.

"Well he might have left some . . ."

Jessie searched, but could not find the word. She looked over at me.

"You know, in the Navajo way, when somebody dies you're not supposed to handle anything that they have used, or things they used to touch, or where they slept, or this type of thing. A place where a person dies you're supposed to burn down, or leave it. They should not have entered that place. If you have to enter that place you have a prayer and a song or something like that. See, if you have something like a spoon, where he has been touching it, and you touch it and you could eat something without washing your hands. Well, that might be something else too."

"What if he had gone to someone else's house and touched things there?"

"It is the same thing. You see, our way of doing some things, when people has been touching it and then they die, you are supposed to wash it and then collect some plants. Just the Medicine Men knows about which ones.

Then you sprinkle the plants over it before you can even use it again."

"Is that if they came in your house just before they died, or a long time before?"

"A year, maybe less; no longer. One of my dad's nieces lives down in Many Farms. She lives in a house that the school built. Her husband died in there and they had to take everything out. They had a song on it and a prayer. Then they had to collect plants just for that certain room. They had to sprinkle the whole house, inside it and outside it. That's the only way they could stay in it."

"Do you go in it now?"

She nodded.

It had been a long and in many ways a painful day, but a good one. Jessie and I drove down to her camp at the base of the mountain.

Rodeo

RODEOS are the main summer fun on the Reservation, there being no movie houses, golf courses, trout streams, or swimming places. There is usually a rodeo every weekend; people crowd into pickups and drive for a hundred miles, often more, to attend.

For the spectators it is a day of dust and candy apples, of ice in your soda pop instead of having it hot and sticky the way it gets sitting around in the camps. It is also a day of watching cousins and friends being bumped and usually dumped by an underfed and angry horse or Brahma bull. Somebody may have a Polaroid camera and sell prints for three dollars.

For the animals, it is a day of being driven halfway across the Reservation, from wherever the suppliers keep their ranches of rodeo stock, in beat-up red-slat trucks, mashed in with too many other animals. It's being shoved in a chute with a hemp rope cinched hard across the scrotum, jabbed with an electric prod when the bell clangs and the gate is thrown open, and simultaneously being gouged by the spurs of a nervous cowboy who knows the harder his animal bucks the more points he will gather, assuming he stays on.

For the Indian cowboy it is a day of glamour and glory, or of disappointment, a lot of bruises and maybe broken bones.

At the Annual Rough Rock Rodeo Jessie and I perched wobbily on the fences. The sun beat down and my camera straps ground bits of the blowing sand into my sunburned shoulders. Trotting down the chutes came a black, hard looking bull named King. John Nez, a friend of Jessie's who often competed in rodeos, said that King had not been ridden in 187 tries.

"When somebody sees his name beside that bull he starts sweatin'," John said; "he's tough, really strong. He jerks you around. You've got to get ahead of him. It's all balance. If he gets ahead and you fall behind then he's gonna start jerkin' you and you start getting tight. And off you go."

After two loudspeaker calls, King's rider had not yet appeared. Then a handsome young man with shoulder-length hair and a band of sweat-stained leather around his head came across the arena. He was wearing a worn leather vest with four ball-point pens in a pocket. He appeared confident and calm. The crowd cheered as he climbed the side of the chute and settled down on King. The gate flew open; the bull felt the prods, the spurs, the jerking. He heaved three times and the rider hit the ground. The crowd went wild with excitement and the announcer, in Navajo, egged them on. Several young boys ran to the fence shouting, "Sonny Jim! Sonny Jim!" They reached out for a touch. Sonny Jim dusted himself off and walked over to the boys, ball-point pens intact.

Jessie told me that Sonny Jim is a cowboy hero to the young kids and a hero of Indian rights to many adults. A poem story written by four of her students begins:

FIRST BOOK OF SONNY JIM
Chapter 1
By Bobby Benally

Sonny Jim is like a hippie. He has long hair with an old head band around his red head. Sonny Jim lives in Gallup. . . . He has white old cowboy boots, with spurs He is a brave man, he is not afraid of all kinds of bull. . . .

In the chapters that follow the hero works his way downhill from broken bones to wife beating, but the *First Book's* last lines sum the man up simply and well:

Sonny Jim is a cowboy. He has a good horses. He is good on bull.

I later met Sonny Jim at the tribal fairgrounds and once in the big grocery store at Window Rock, where Jessie's family and hundreds of others meet every few Saturdays. Sonny Jim is not a Navajo; he is a Klamath from Washington State, but he married a Navajo and lives on her land between Gallup and Window Rock. He told me he is on the verge of being dishonored because he has spoken so actively against rodeo judges giving higher points to their own clan members. He predicted that, although he was winning most events now, he would start losing because of the resentment he had kindled. Sonny Jim is not sure he likes rodeos anyway. "I am working with a rodeo committee," he said, "to start a series of pow-wows, with traditional Indian stick games and running games, Indian foods and dances, bareback races; the things we have always done. I don't see any reason why we don't get away from the Anglo-type activities at these weekend gatherings, and also funnel the money back to the people instead of paying an Anglo animal supplier $800 a day to use his battered stock, for example."

Recently the Rodeo Association adopted new rules for the calf-roping event. It was difficult for old-time cowboys to adjust to the new style in an action requiring the split-second tying of three feet of a bellowing, squirming calf.

Jessie told me of Phillip Benally, a gentle, sad-eyed man in his middle fifties, and an expert cowboy. A few days before the Rough Rock rodeo, while he was practicing the new style, Phillip, with one end of his rope attached to the pommel of his saddle, galloped after and lassoed a fleeing calf. His little quarterhorse stopped instantly, Phillip leapt for the calf, knocked it to the dust, and started whipping the rope around the calf's thrashing feet. He gave a signal for the horse to step backward to jerk the rope taut. Phillip worked awkwardly, with a flicker of hesitation caused by the new style. The horse yanked back as Phillip's hands were still finishing a knot and the rope snapped off two fingers.

The highway was about a forty-five minute drive from the practice ground and the Public Health Service an hour further. After the Health Service doctor examined Phillip's hand he said it was impossible to sew the fingers back on. Phillip and his family pleaded but the doctor said it would be futile to try. They left, took the fingers, and drove 120 miles to another hospital. The doctor there said he could have done it if Phillip had got there sooner, but now it was too late. Phillip said, as his son translated it:

"But they are me. They are part of me, of my body. They must be joined to make me whole again."

The fingers lay there in front of him and the doctor could not help them become part of him again. On the eve of the rodeo, a ceremony was held for the death of Phillip's fingers.

Schools

THE SUN was very low. Black Mountain was shrouded in deep purple, and the light had almost gone. As the sun dropped behind the mountain a scarlet line marked the horizon, shimmering as a dust storm blew between it and us. Behind us, Jessie's eight-year-old nephew, Freddie, sat on his father's horse. Both he and the horse were hunched over, their backs to the stinging wind, as they brought in the sheep. Freddie, the earth, the sky, and the air were all in muted blues, purples, and somber blue-browns.

Jessie and I went into the house she uses for a summer bedroom and lit the two Coleman lanterns on the stove. Jessie's summer bedroom has three beds, several mattresses on the floor, a wardrobe, and a bureau with an overbearingly large mirror pasted with family photographs and mementos. The mirror reflected the lanterns and somewhat brightened the room, but outside darkness closed in on the camp and only the bleating of the sheep corralled behind the house broke the vast silence. Jessie started spinning the grey wool she and the family had been shearing. She pulled a tape from her pocketbook, put it on the tape recorder, and turned the volume high. Waylon Jenning's voice protested, his guitar thumped, and Jessie turned the scratchy sound up higher to etch her mood a little more deeply into the darkness.

Jessie says that Waylon Jennings sings songs that reach right inside her and cry her cries. When he sings about Donna, Jessie wishes she were named Donna. "Navajo kids think about loneliness a lot," she said, as Waylon Jennings sang:

> And it took me back to something
> that I'd lost somewhere,
> somehow along the way.
> I headed back for home
> and somewhere faraway
> a lonely bell was ringing. . .

"Some people," Jessie said, "some of them, it seems that they just forget this and that, and then they forget their language. I don't want to do that. I want to stay with my own people and speak the way they do. My cousin went to summer school at Navajo Community College and got enough credits and now she teaches on the other side of the mountain. But most of the schools are terrible here on the Reservation.

"I was going to public school at Kayenta all this time. The public school is slightly more human than the Bureau of Indian Affairs schools, but you can't live there. I had to go over and live in a trailer with my aunt in Kayenta. The bus had to go so far to get us. It drove from Shonto, Mexican Water, Cow Springs, Oljetoh, Dinnehotso, and it would take two hours because some of those kids lived forty-five miles away. They were an Arizona public school but they never taught us about Navajos. The only history we had was from the white man's point of view. They had a Department of Interior book in the library called *Soldier and Brave*, and I wondered if they had any Navajo history. I looked up Canyon de Chelly and do you know what it said about that battle? Something like, 'The Navajos, an aggressive and hostile tribe of Indians, were finally subdued in this beautiful National Monument.'

"So my last semester I decided to transfer to the BIA school at Fort Wingate. I didn't know anyone there; it was pretty awful. At BIA they tell you to do this and do that, you know, like you're a slave.

"Everyone washes their face at the same time, then you make up your bed and line up for breakfast—in high school! You still have to line up for everything, two by two. You march to class and sit boy, girl, boy, girl all the way down the line. You are punished if you speak Navajo. That's saddest for the little kids. They have to start living in a boarding school when they are just five or six. They don't know English and they are so scared."

As Jessie spoke I remembered my first morning on the Reservation, years ago. I had got up before sunrise and sat outside on the wooden doorstep of my hogan and watched the stars, which gave no sign of yielding to the dawn. Then very rapidly the horizon filled with low deep-red streaks, long ribbons of full, intense light. They climbed higher and higher, and I saw that a corral and stable were between my door and the sunrise. There were about six horses there and they began stirring in the cold morning. I could see their breath in the glow of dawn and I tried to imagine being a Navajo child and growing up with this sunrise being as ordinary a thing as a fire engine is to a city child. I tried to imagine being taken to a BIA school and packed into a dormitory where dawn comes abruptly when a switch is flipped and your bed is bathed in a sickly-green fluorescent light.

"At Rough Rock it's different," Jessie continued. "That's why I work there now. The kids go home every weekend and if they don't live way up on the mountain they can go home every night. They learn to read and write Navajo first, then when they are eight or nine they learn English as a second language by using puppets and games. After that the classes are in English but every room has Navajo aides and mothers helping the kids, helping them be proud to be a Navajo.

"They teach weaving and silversmithing as well as things like mechanics or arithmetic, science or photography. Parents take turns living in the dorms to do the mending and stuff like that and to tell stories at bedtime so the kids will learn our legends.

"And the kids learn about gathering herbs for ceremonies and making dyes. The high school had a field trip to San Francisco. They went to Fisherman's Wharf and rode the cable cars and they brought back sea water for the medicine men to use in their ceremonies.

"Navajo mothers used to hide their children when they saw a white man coming because they didn't want their children to be treated the way the government did. They took my uncle off to school way over near Albuquerque when he was nine years old. He and two other boys ran away to come home, and people chased them and they were scared, but they got back here."

Jessie put down her spinning, went over to the bureau and picked up a piece of government-green cardboard. "I ripped this off the trading-post wall yesterday. It made me so hollow and lonely to read it:

FINAL SHIPMENT
Intermountain
Sept. 16, be at Chinle Brdg. School, at
5 p.m.
For those who missed Aug. 26 Shipment

That shipment is the shipment of Navajo children, even four- and five-year olds, to the BIA school up in Colorado. Can you see how little children could start out being lonely in the white man's world?"

Jessie must have thought she had said enough. She stopped talking, looked at me with a faint smile, and turned her attention back to Waylon Jennings:

And it echoed through the canyon
like the disappearin' dream
of yesterday

Silently asking her permission, I borrowed her flashlight, nodded goodnight, and set out under a dark desert sky for the Whitesheep hogan in which I was staying. Waylon Jenning's singing, fainter and fainter, followed me into the night.

Poems by Students, Rough Rock School

Myself

As I sit in class
I daydream instead of listening
I get restless instead of learning
I get sleepy instead of writing
I get a headache instead of working
I look at comics instead of answering questions
When it's time to go,
I'm the first one out
No wonder I'm dumb

—ANONYMOUS

"poem"

you can look into my face
and all you see is a very old ugly face.
    but I can see in my eyes
    a great handsome young man.
you can look into my face
and all you can see is a sad lonesome young man.
    but I can see in my eyes
    a happy cheerful young man.
you can look into my face
and all you can see is mean.
    but I can see in my eyes
    a nice, gentle, generous young man.

—MIKE TODACHINE

Untitled

There is a woman with a camera
She is trying to take a profile
Aaagh she has taken my profile
I know who she is
she is from the FBI
Now they shall take me away
Then they shall put me away
just cause I forgot
to clean my room.
CLANG

—CHE-BONNIE TSINAHJINNIE

Untitled

I seem to be working and thinking
But I am really running through a meadow.

I seem to be a canyon with love and happiness filling me
But I am really a mountain reaching up for more.

I seem to be a sparkling smooth running brook cool and refreshing
But I'm really a raging wild river with rapids.

I seem to be a raging hot day
But I'm really dawn and dusk joined together to make
            the stars come out.

I seem to be growing up
But I am really a frisky clumsy puppy.

I seem to be a graceful ballet dancer
But really I can't chew gum and walk at the same time.

I seem to be insane
But really the whole world is insane and I am the only sane one.

I seem to be a dried up prune
But really I am Hulleah.

I seem to be like the moon floating alone lazy like
But really I am a cricket trying not be eaten tonight.

I seem to be here and always will be
But really I'm going to go—pop!
                    —HULLEAH TSINAHJINNIE

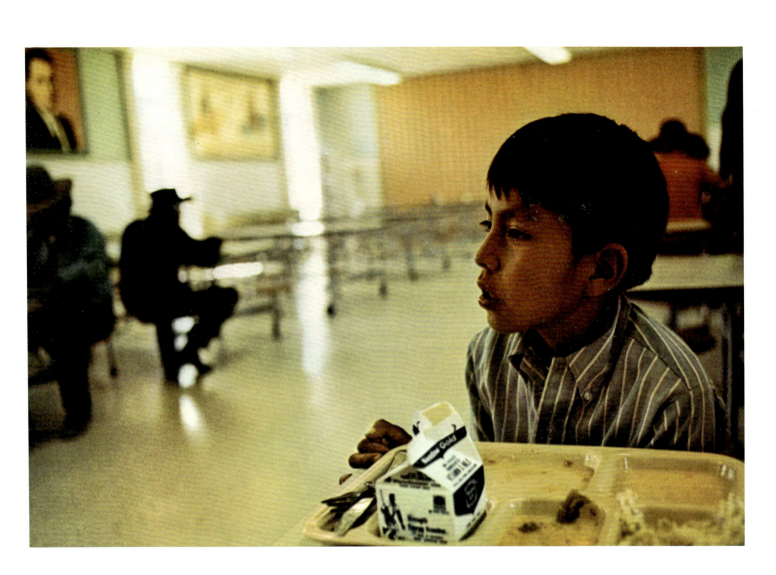

Classroom

JESSIE is a teacher's aide in Pat Belletto's classroom. It looks more like a clubhouse than a school. Children of all ages drift in and sit around in small groups with the regular students. The phonograph plays softly. Children are in clusters of three or four working quietly, reading, curled up on a rug cutting collages from old Christmas paper. There are two looms; rugs have been begun on them. Several large pieces of fabric have been tie-dyed by the students and are hanging from the ceiling, billowing like purple and gray thunderheads. Jessie sits behind a semicircle of tables sorting out beads and working on a yellowish-green lacy crystal necklace. Her cyclamen jacket brightens the corner which is already cheery. Her own table is a goldenrod yellow and behind her are string sculptures glued to red, pink and orange construction paper. When the children start horsing around Jessie yells at them in Navajo, guttural and deep. There are five or six work sections in the room. The other tables are painted vibrant red and ripelemon yellow. One is cluttered with chalk, toothpicks, glue, a saw. Brightly painted boxes are stacked with supplies to make frybread and popcorn. Jessie's kids have a weekly popcorn or frybread sale to raise money to buy beads. There are cans of pineapple juice and apple juice and an electric frying pan. Jessie is one of the sensitive and artistic bead makers in the community and she is teaching the children how. She can design pins or necklaces in her head, much the way her mother designs rugs, and her cousin Leonard Honie designs silver. Jessie made me a large, round pin with a sunburst design in the middle—she just started and the design came to her head and grew from there.

Jessie likes the children and they like her. They all call her Jessie in class and hang around her beading table and try to learn some of her skill.

Once, when we went back to class after gym, some kids from another class had come in the room to help themselves to beads and had overturned the nine or ten bead boxes on Jessie's table as they fled in haste. Thousands of small glass beads, red, pinks, silvers, two or three shades of greens, long beads, round ones, sparkles and matte blacks were jumbled across the floor. Jessie sighed and got a broom. She and the kids spent the next three days sorting colors and putting them in their proper boxes. To pick up one of those tiny beads you need a willowy needle with which you push on one side of the bead to flip it up on the tip of the needle, then move it to the box. Each of those thousands of mixed-up beads was moved that way.

When Jessie makes a lacy chain of loops and flowers each bead is secured to the one before or after it so that if the thread should break, one bead, maybe two or three, but no more, fall off. Yet I've never seen a thread showing on anything she has made.

Jessie teaches Navajo, reading and writing, to groups of eight-, nine-, and ten-year olds. She also tutors in English reading and mathematics and poetry. One winter there were prolonged fogs. Jessie says the world became a fairyland. The fog made the trees damp and at night the moisture would freeze. In the morning the fog would still be rolling in, making the world white, cold, almost invisible. As sun warmed the land the ice melted and the twigs twinkled and sparkled and flashed through the gray air. She asked her students to write about the fog. One of them, Sylvester, wrote,

> In the morning
> there is no world
> when there is fog.

First Jessie teaches the children their numbers from one to ten and their colors. After they learn numbers they go on to reading. Little books have been made up by the Navajo Curriculum Center at the school. The one Jessie loved was about a boy who walked outside with some freshly cooked frybread. The boy meets a big boy named Emerson who snatches the frybread. Just then a wild dog sneaks in behind the boys and swallows the bread. They separate and go back in their own directions—neither one happy. They just walk away cussing the dog. The children were supposed to make up a name for the little boy and most gave him their own name.

The pupils gave a Christmas play last year, "The Purple and Green Three Headed Monster That Ate Up

Untitled

To kill is like
> *Hatred.*
tθ Love is like
> *a beautiful day (sometimes)*
To fight is like
> *Jealousy.*
To talk is like
> *Barking.*
To run is like
> *Commotion.*
To sit in a classroom is like running on a escalator.
You get nowhere
> *in this World.*

—LARRY BENALLY

All the Snow." Jessie explained that they had to change the title to give three heads to the monster because: "We had this monster costume that three kids were in. The two kids in the back didn't like not seeing. We changed the story, so they could be heads, too."

Jessie helps take the children to physical education class. During a kickball game in the gym she became engrossed and yelled polyglot instructions: "Truman, *doo hanii* second *basej, jool ahilanda ei doodago aaji bit nidiiyeeda.*" She was telling Truman to throw the ball to second base, for which there is no word in Navajo, or throw it to someone else but not just stand there holding it. Both Jessie and the children switch from English to Navajo, sentence by sentence, word by word, whichever seems to express what they have to say more accurately. This always amazes me because they are switching from thought pattern to thought pattern as well, no small accomplishment for a child categorized by an inspector from the U.S. Office of Education as a Title I child—that is, a child who can't read English as well as someone his age in Baltimore.

A Public Health Service doctor was far more obtuse than the Office of Education inspector: Some time ago Rosemary Jim, a teenager, had partial kidney failure. Jessie and her teacher took her repeatedly to the PHS office in Chinle. When her condition was finally diagnosed, the doctor said they were just wasting time.

"We'll cure her and then she'll go home. These Indians just don't take care of themselves after you've finished." They refused to treat her. They wouldn't release the kidney machine for her to use. The doctor told the Anglo teacher that it was just better if she died. When Rosemary walked out, the teacher asked, "Where am I? In outer space? What kind of people are these?" Finally Rosemary went to Denver and she is now doing all right.

Jessie put up a clan chart for the children in her class.

"A lot of the kids didn't even know they were in the same clans. Mary Ann Redhair, she's the one they used to hate a lot. I mean, the way I see it, they treated her real mean, and here the meanest ones were the ones that were related to her and they didn't even know it. I told them about it and now they aren't even mean to her any more.

"If there is a Squaw Dance and someone wants to dance with a girl, he has to be sure she's not one of his relatives. It has to be someone not related before he can touch her. So many people in this community are related, and some of them here still goes around with one of their relatives, I don't know what their parents say, but everyone talks about them behind their backs. I've heard some people are even married to their brothers or their cousins in other districts, that's what I heard. But their children will have crooked faces or will be sick.

"Even if you love someone in your clan you can't do anything about it. We talk to the little kids about this, because once they have the habit of doing something they don't want to quit. When they grow up they *have* to know what a person's clan is, I tell them all the time. Older people makes fun of you behind your back if you marry someone related to you. Your children will have bad eyes and bad blood.

"It is really hard to live in a community when the older people talk about you."

With hardly a pause to indicate it, there was a sudden change of direction in her thinking. If it was hard to live in the community, it would be harder still to leave it.

"I think," Jessie said, "the kids from here will want to stay here and live."

Chapter House

THE NAVAJO NATION is divided by the Navajo Tribe into districts, and the districts into chapters. Jessie told me about a meeting at the chapter house built in her community: "Last week, a lot of the old people from the community and Many Farms and Chinle came and they asked my dad to come over, too. I drove him there and he told me about it afterwards. Lorraine Thomas had been seein' Johnny Lee for several years, she even said she had a little boy of his. They are in the same clan, Todachine, and the chapter asked my dad to come because he is Todachine clan, too. Lorraine and her husband and some of their kids were there and her parents and her husband's parents, too. And Johnny Lee and his wife and their parents. Lorraine wanted money from Johnny and she even said she was going to have another baby. Her husband works at the power plant at Page and he didn't even know all of this was going on.

"The old people listened to her telling just everything, then they said that she should not have been foolin' around and if she did and then she wanted money she should have come to the chapter much earlier. They were all gossiping about her and making fun of her. Johnny Lee is not going to get a divorce because his mother doesn't want him to and he has seven children to support already. After the meeting he just disappeared and he's hiding way back up in the mountain. Lorraine's husband said he was going to kill him if he can find him, and he's about the biggest man I know. Lorraine is already gone. Her husband is working at the school now, and he is taking care of the kids. She won't come back."

The chapter house is concerned with more than community discipline. For instance, it has ten-day projects that give men and women money to work for ten days.

"The council man finds out who really needs some extra money," Jessie said, "and he goes to the Tribe at Window Rock and gets some. The community needed firewood this winter and the men worked for ten days gathering and cutting it and they got paid. The people came and loaded their pickups with wood for the winter. Ladies weave for ten days. If they take longer to finish the rug, they still get paid for only ten days. The pay used to be $96 but now it is $109. Every year it will go up, I don't know how many per cent that is. They turn the rug back to the chapter house and there is a lady who stays there to collect them and then she takes them to a rug auction. Then whatever they get they put in the bank and there is money for some sort of emergency. My mom did it last month. Usually they have somebody who goes around to the different homes to see if the ladies are weaving when they are supposed to be. Some traditional Navajos don't approve of the chapter house projects. They say the people wait and do a project instead of coming and working just to help a neighbor."

This is rough country
God made it,
Man named it,
Nature owns it,
Time has toned it,
This is rough country.
—JOE LAKE

Questions

WE WOULD often walk a long while in silence. Now and then Jessie would break the silence with a question, such as, "After you were divorced for six years, and you got married again, how did your husband feel about your children?" She asked some questions again and again, trying to pull my answers into the perspective of her life. Since she had not lived in my world as I had lived in hers, my answers must sometimes have been very difficult to understand. Her interest in my life was one thing not concerned with her community or her people that we kept trying to share.

Not long ago, as we were returning to her camp in her pickup and listening to the news, there was a bulletin about the American Indian Movement demonstration at Wounded Knee. I asked her what she thought about militant Indians. She shrugged her shoulders and said that she did not think that could happen among the Navajos at Rough Rock. People were too busy worrying about their families, their livestock, and their clans. Then she leaned over and turned up the radio so loudly that if I had asked any more questions she wouldn't have heard them anyway. The pickup bounced and heaved along the road, the desert air resounding as Jessie's favorite country and Western singer, Waylon Jennings, sang of his long lost love.

Kee Begay

WHEN THE Grazing Committee was holding its annual cattle inspection at Kitsillie, I went to the mountain alone, Jessie not wanting to come, to meet her uncle, Kee Begay. He was driving his stock from the family camp, about ten miles from John Hadley's to the inspection corral. It would be a dusty, hot drive, lasting almost all day.

Kee has a broad head and a massive torso perched on thin legs that propel him through a life of seemingly boundless energy. At night Kee operates the drag line, an overburden stripper, the largest machine at the Peabody Coal Company strip mine at the northern end of the mountain. He has operated every machine and has held every job at the mine. He is one of the highest paid men there as well. He got off work at dawn, drove several hours along the mesa to his mother's home, and there joined his teenage daughters. They had spent the previous week riding back into the woodlands to rout out the cattle for the drive.

I found him unhappy because the drive would take meat off the animals. Now the cattle were already balking and being turned by the bull, who did not want to leave his familiar territory. Kee's black, jumpy stallion skittered sideways and they disappeared in dust. Kee shouting directions to six of his children to keep the straggling calves moving. In English he shouted to me to keep the left flank of the herd moving with my Volkswagen and to make sure none of the cattle dropped off into the Oriabi wash, a fifteen-foot drop just to my left. Arid wooded hills rose on both sides of the hot dusty valley. The calves were bawling for their mothers, opening their eyes wide and showing the whites in fright. One of the daughters rode a Shetland pony whose foal trotted along behind, nursing whenever the herd paused.

After several hours we rode up a dry wash that branched from the Oriabi and led to the Begay sheep camp, tucked among the trees and rocks. It looked lush for the desert, with corn and potatoes growing in a nearby garden. Several small children stopped playing ball to crowd impatiently beside the front door, where Mrs. Begay was cutting a watermelon. Kee leaned down to tell me: "Never cut a melon with the tip of the knife. It is bad luck." He laughed and asked if I thought I would ever learn all the things I must not do.

The house had several rooms, and the women had cooked an enormous lunch for everyone in the big pine-paneled kitchen. There were big windows and a long table covered in red-flowered oilcloth, hardly visible under the pots of pinto beans, platters of fresh mutton ribs, fried intestines chopped in five-inch lengths, frybread, sliced watermelon, baskets of oranges, and two large chipped enamel coffee pots, one with coffee, one with tea. The women stood and watched us eat, refilling our plates every time they began to empty.

The ribs had been grilled over cedar coals in large pieces. We sliced off as much as we wanted and chewed the delicious meat down to the bone. I've never found their equal in the city. In most Navajo homes, the uncooked mutton is hung in the shade house, a stack of cedar boughs, pieces of plywood, and more cedar boughs piled against a rectangular room-sized frame. The cedar keeps the sun out but breezes filter through and cool the house. Flies and bees filter through, too, swarming around the cheesecloth wrapping the meat. After several summer days of hanging the meat has a sourish taste. Sometimes I liked it and sometimes I didn't. Fresh mutton is sweet and juicy—and a luxury.

After lunch, we continued the cattle drive in Kee's truck and his daughter, Marlane, rode his stallion. He talked freely.

"That girl can ride like a man. She can rope and bulldog and she can break any horse to the saddle. Her man was killed in Vietnam last year, so she is back here helping me with the animals. She is a wonderful daughter."

Marlane was twenty-three and tall. Her face was full and strong. Her hair hung almost to her waist. It swung from side to side and shone in the sunlight as the stallion galloped off to join the cattle. She didn't smile much, but her eyes were gentle.

Kee told me he left home at fifteen and worked in Oregon as a translator for the railroads. He is fluent in English and is very aware of the Anglo way of thinking. His wife, who is Director of the cafeteria at the Rough Rock School, speaks English very well, too. Kee explained that Navajos often think Anglos are outrageously pushy and forward; they ask so many questions they seem to have no respect for a person's privacy. He says white people often think of Navajos as passive, shy, and rude, but he feels that it is just a clash of cultures, not a personal thing.

The branding corral was crowded with people and animals. A few men watched from the fence, but most were working—roping, tackling, inoculating, shouting for branding irons. There was much teasing, and the older men laughed at the younger ones when they made lassoing mistakes. Kee's wife and sons helped hold the calves down for branding. His mother joined the older women, who were heating the irons in a cedar fire, running them to impatient branders, and stopping only to cut more firewood to keep the coals hot. The women, many with no teeth, their drawn faces wrapped in calico scarves, were laughing as they worked, delighted by the occasion that brought together all the families from their isolated camps on the mountain.

I saw many old acquaintances. One was a medicine man some people say is ninety. He once broke all traditions and showed me a string game in the summer, over the protests of his bewildered great-grandchildren. He laughed, shrugged his shoulders, scooped up a kitten—kittens always seem to be around—and tossed it at the noisiest little boy. That was funny enough to the children to end their protest. They began making cats' cradles, bishops' hats, and faces for my camera.

Except for the poor steer that had been cut too deeply in the de-horning and would bleed to death that day, the branding was successful. At dusk the tired Begay family began the long drive back to their cattle camp.

Witches

WHILE we were riding in his truck Kee Begay told me more than once that if a Navajo gets too successful or makes too much money he will be disliked, gossiped about, and feared in his community. I suggested that perhaps it was often like that with Anglos. He said emphatically that it was quite different for Navajos, but that I wouldn't understand.

But I did understand. The subject was too private to risk discussing it, but I knew that he was talking about Navajo witches. Navajos, I had learned from Jessie, believe that certain evil men or women can, with witchcraft, cause illness or bring death to those they hate, or those they are hired to harm.

In daylight witches are ordinary people, sheepherders, miners, politicians, or administrators. At night, they stalk their victims and frighten them with signs: scratching on windows just before dawn morning after morning; with supernatural powers, running as fast as a horse or a pickup truck, trying to sprinkle the victim with the dust of a corpse or some other horrible and forbidden thing, usually something associated with the dead. The victim will then die or have a serious accident unless he has a ceremony to undo the harm. At night, when witches roam, they wear the skin of a coyote or wolf and are often referred to as wolf-men. Wolf-men cast a spell on dogs at a hogan so that even the boldest watchdog falls silent when the witch comes, and cannot warn the family. Sometimes witches actually kill a victim directly.

One man I know told of the night he was driving his pickup on the road to Many Farms. He heard a bumping noise and stopped. While inspecting the tires, he swung his flashlight across the desert. The beam was reflected in two eyes, green rather than the cod-liver-oil color of a dog's. He turned the beam back on the eyes again and the animal behind the eyes stood on its hind legs and began walking toward him. He bolted for the truck, locked the doors, and sped off down the rutted road. The animal calmly ran faster and faster until it was even with the truck. Then it jumped into the back and stared through the back window. Seeing the face in the rear-view mirror, the man was terrified. Wildly though he drove over the desert road, he was unable to shake the face—until he reached a paved road and some street lights. The face was gone.

I was told that when a witch is near you can sense instantly a clammy, cold, weird feeling. In remote camps, when Navajos feel frightened at night they have no way to push the darkness back. A lantern casts too many shadows; a flashlight beam is so feeble that it only deepens the surrounding darkness and accentuates the helplessness and terror of the hunted.

Witches and other manifestations of magic are not easily understood by those who don't have to put up with them. There is much talk about witches. Belief in them seems universal in Navajos. I asked Jessie a little about them.

"You have to always stay in the middle," she told me. "You want to have enough sheep and things so you will always have food and clothes but not be so rich that those things happen. Other people gets so cruel and jealous that they start getting somebody to witch you. Usually you are witched by someone in your family or clan. Even your own close relatives can do that to you. Like we have relatives way up on the mountain and in Crystal and over in Kayenta and some real real close. Whenever they think that we are getting too rich or they get jealous —if we have more cattle or sheep or even pickups—they hire someone to warn us. I don't really know how they find one."

She waited a long time.

"I don't know how to find a witch. I haven't done that yet." She laughed to make sure I understood that she was joking.

"I wouldn't know if I could do it or not. I always think about these things, too . . . I don't see how they could stand to do it. They could be giving up their life, or something like that. People say when you have been witched you have a sing or peyote meeting and you can find out right away who is the witch and the person who

hired him. They tell you the distance where that person is living and what the person looks like. That's all you know. But you know that you have a relative who lives that far from you and who dresses like that. The Navajo people have about thirty-five different ceremonies and most all of them are about witches or ghosts."

Then, as I had hoped so long that she might, Jessie told me the kind of thing Navajos hardly ever tell Anglos; but the news was sad.

"I have been very scared at my house lately. Someone has been bothering us. My father is away for five days, and we can't sleep. One by one, all seven of our dogs have disappeared. Some of those dogs we have had for years and some were puppies. One of our dogs was a real good one, too. Like when someone or something was coming, he knows. He can't lie to us. He barks and we go outside and there would be a horse or a dog or a cat or something. He always barked. Now he is gone. That never happened before and I don't know why they are missing. Late at night it sounds like a pebble is being thrown up on the roof, near the smoke hole. It rolls down and we never hear it hit the ground. That happened over and over. And other things have happened, too. My sister-in-law came to visit us, and late at night when she left both the front tires fell off her pickup."

A witch can shoot his victim with a dartlike object that carries something connected with a dead person and is able by magic to penetrate a hogan wall. Or he can get something that belongs to the person he is witching and cast a spell over it. Jessie said that is why she never hangs laundry outside the house, and why, when she brushes Lolita's hair, she burns the loose hair left in the brush.

"When you spit on the ground," she warned, "take your foot and spread it out or someone can cut it out of the ground and use it on you."

Various plants, known only to medicine men or very old people who have become herbalists, help protect against witches. If a person is convinced that he knows

who is after him, he can have an Enemy Way, sometimes called a Squaw Dance, performed over him. After the first night of chanting, a group of mounted Navajos ride to another hogan several miles away. One rider carries a small bundle tied to a pole in which there is something from the supposed witch—a fingernail clipping, a few pieces of hair, a piece of clothing. At a second hogan the group is met by more mounted Indians and a mock battle takes place. This symbolizes evil being turned from the patient to the witch. Jessie says this ceremony is like a medicine man's shooting an evil bullet to the witch or to the person who hired the witch. Navajos believe that this cure ceremony will cause the witch to die a bloody and painful death within a year.

If someone in the community has an unusual accident, most people shrug it off: "Well, he must have been practicing witchcraft." There have been two deaths in Jessie's community within the past year that have been blamed on witchcraft. The people say that several years ago the area had one of the worst blizzards in history because a witch was run over by a pickup but was not killed. He spent a whole day in agony and he used all his supernatural spirits to call the weather to harm the people.

An Anglo friend of Jessie's told me that a nearby school had been witched.

"There had been several small accidents," he said, "—a broken arm or leg. Someone had been walking through the dorms at night scaring the children, and a number of people had reported seeing a wolf-man. One night the dorm parents saw him and chased him almost a mile. He disappeared over by the corral. They wrecked their car."

The Anglo friend's house is on the school compound. Once, when his wife was out of town on a field trip and he was working at home in the darkroom, he had turned out all the lights in the house, turned up his tape set, and had begun printing. Suddenly there was a silence. A deep chill ran through him. He rushed to the kitchen. Through the window, out of the corner of his eye, he saw a large white dog running—on two feet. It faded as he looked at it. The same night, the woman who lived behind him was alone with her kids and suddenly she felt a terrifying chill. She wanted to call Jessie's friend but she found she was too frightened, so she spent the night huddled with her children in an inner room of her house.

There was unrest around the school, so the School Board, without telling any of the staff, called in a Hand Trembler, the diagnostician of the Navajo religion. After a ritual that included songs, prayers, and violent physical trembling, the diagnostician led the director to an area in the schoolyard, pointed to a spot of earth, and told the director to dig. He unearthed a can with six stick figures scratched on the side, each figure having an accident. Inside the can were pieces of hair, a piece of a dress hem, and lint from the dryers at the dorms. Four of the accidents had already happened.

The Hand Trembler also prophesied a violent fight in the school between a Navajo and an Anglo. The next day the Navajo librarian became exasperated with a young Anglo teacher who wore blue jeans to class. This annoyed the librarian so much that he started screaming at her, grabbed her by the hair, and began jerking it wildly.

The Director hired a medicine man who held a ceremony for the school. A Peyote Ceremony was held, too. The whole school gathered as the Peyote Chief prayed for the school, for Mother's Day (which was imminent), for the American flag, and for the students.

In the hierarchy of Navajo healers, the medicine man is the top. He has supernatural gifts and must endure long training. I photographed Frank Wilson training a man and a woman for the Beautyway—the first time, I was told, that ingredients of ceremonial baskets had been photographed, or elements of the training. He showed me the notebook he used to pass the ceremony to his students. They all spoke only Navajo, but they did not read or write it. The ceremony was depicted by a series of stick figures, cornstalks, random dots, and other shapes. It was not unlike an Anasazi drawing that Jessie and I discovered on the face of a large, flat rock on the mountain.

The Hand Trembler, as diagnostician, goes into a trance and with his supernatural insight determines what ceremony is needed to cure the patient, and what medicine man would be best for the job. The Hand Trembler brings temporary relief until a medicine man can be afforded. He has no supernatural powers.

Jessie explained the Peyote Ceremony as well. Most people in the Rough Rock Community are members of the Native American Church, or Peyote Church. The church is strictly against immoral behavior. It also opposes liquor, mainly because of the shame alcohol has brought the Navajos. Christianity, guns, and whiskey are the three bad things the Navajo blame on the Anglos. Those three things have thrown The People's harmony out of balance.

"The church has dealt with guns," she said. "They've dealt with Christianity by taking the best parts of it and incorporating them with the Navajo way. And now they are dealing with liquor."

In dealing with liquor, the church uses peyote, the bitter-tasting cactus bud containing mescaline.

"With peyote," Jessie said, "the church believes that members can get over inhibitions and people can say what is really troubling them. It is a purifier as well, which is important in the Navajo way.

"If a drunk comes to a church meeting, the people don't reject him like the missionary up at the chapter house. They'll ask, 'Why do you drink?' This person will soon just pour out all his reasons. Then they all talk about it among friends, people he's known all his life. After the whole thing, people say, 'Well, we love you and we'll stick with you.' If you run out and get drunk again, everybody knows it, of course. If you want to come to the meeting, they welcome you again, and they'll stick with you for a long, long time trying to get you to be better.

"The meetings start about eight o'clock and last all night. Usually they are held in a large hogan, a forty-footer, or a special tent always used for the meeting. It depends who the Peyote Chief is. Everyone sits around the wall, sits for a long time. They pass peyote and chew it. It's a powder or buttons, usually buttons. Only members can take peyote. They carry cards. The National President in the Dakotas or somewhere has to sign the card. If you took peyote, you could be arrested if you weren't a member of the church. The buds really taste bitter. You sort of ding-a-ling for a while until you start getting expanded. Mainly, you see beautiful colors in the fire. Then you wander off into the bushes to vomit and get purified. Just before the sun comes up, everybody runs toward the sun till it comes over the horizon, especially those that they are praying for. It's a long run. Everybody is tired and sweaty. Usually the next day everybody sacks out all day and sleeps. That's why Navajos have trouble holding steady, Anglo-type jobs—that and the five- and nine-day ceremonies.

"You know those pickups with decals of an eagle on them?" Jessie asked. "Those are members of the Peyote Church. The eagle is its national symbol."

The Peyote Church reminded Jessie of witches. She told me that if, on the fourth day of an Enemy Way ceremony, a witch is discovered, the Peyote Church tells him to repent. If he doesn't, he will die a miserable and often brutal death, an outcast from the traditional Navajo way. If he repents, he will still die, but he can lead a good life for the year he has left, and die cleared of his guilt.

Harmony

THE MORE songs and prayers a Navajo knows, Jessie said, the more harmonious his life may become. He believes that he is one with nature; he has neither more nor less importance in his world than an antelope, a sunbeam, or a rock. All nature must be in balance for harmony to exist. Without harmony there is sickness and unhappiness. Everything that a Navajo does is influenced by his concept of supernatural forces, ever-present and threatening to destroy harmony.

There are two personal forces: Earth Surface People, ordinary people alive, or dead, as ghosts; and Holy People, powerful, mysterious, legendary, traveling on sunbeams, rainbows, or lightning, and aiding or harming Earth Surface People. One Holy Person lives in each of the four sacred mountains and eight more smaller mountains that are holy, including Black Mountain. That gives The People their protection. When their population increases so much that it forces them to spread beyond the four sacred mountains, they will run into difficulties with nature and will be out of harmony with their god's plans. Their people will come to an end.

When one of the hostile forces breaks the carefully balanced harmony in a person's life, a ceremony must be held to bring back harmony. There are many signs to indicate that harmony has been destroyed. Someone steps on a snake, or is plagued by evil thoughts or bad dreams. Lightning comes frighteningly close or strikes an animal in a herd. Ghosts appear in an animal's shape at night, or as a dark object, sometimes making noises or changing size. An unexplained lump comes on the body. Or a person has fainting spells.

When Jessie's youngest sister, Alice, returned from Tucson one week she had small lumps on her neck, not like welts from an allergy. The Whitesheeps held a ceremony for her in their winter hogan. Only the family and one medicine man were there. Jessie thought Alice had probably eaten mutton that had been bitten by a snake.

When the whole family is on hand, perhaps twice a year, the Whitesheeps hold a Blessing Way Ceremony, just for good hope.

Religion is not an easy subject for Jessie to discuss. Indeed, she tells me there is no word in Navajo for what Anglos call religion. Navajo feelings for their cultural heritage and the supernatural and the balance of harmony they must maintain is so ingrained in their lives, so inseparable from their daily deeds, that there is no way to distinguish life from religion. On an earlier visit, when Jessie was going to buy her pickup, I remember having fretted about her setting out in her brother's truck for Farmington, several hours away, with the down payment of over a thousand dollars cash—saved from more than a year of teaching—in her pocket. She looked at me for a long moment and said quietly, "We have songs for that. I am safe."

Ceremony and song bring safety, but so does the consideration that Navajos give each other. Jessie gave me two examples.

"The School Board runs the school," she said, "but when it does it really considers the financial end of hiring people. One lady got divorced and she had a lot of kids to support. She had a real need. Although there might have been someone more qualified than she was, they hired her because she was from the community. That time it turned out real well. She was really good. But then they hired Wenona Begaye as a parent aide. First of all she was no parent, and second of all she was no aid!"

Then Jessie told me about her brother, Peter.

"Peter is a poet. He lives to talk. That's all he does, is talk and talk and write. He was with the medicine-man program at the school. He knows more about it than anyone up here. But they laid him off because he has been going back and forth to Phoenix."

She was silent for a long time, evidently wondering if she should tell me about Peter's automobile accident.

I had heard gossip of it from everyone, but I sat and waited.

"See, he had an accident last year before summer. Well, they charged him with manslaughter, and he had to go back and forth. We had to do lots of singing and prayers for him.

"They put him on probation. He had to make about six trips to Phoenix. They asked him to come back a certain day and they would say he'd have to come another day. Or he would have to come a certain day before ten, and he'd have to make his trip a day in advance. It got to be too much, keeping his job, and he got laid off.

"So he helped my mom. I guess—I'm not sure—I think they are going to take him back some day.

"If they take him back or not he will be tried in job after job until he can find a place where he can work. During the time he was doing so much travelling, they asked him to write poetry for the school newspaper—the perfect job for him when he was bothered by so much."

The Coal Mine

KEE BEGAY works at the Peabody strip mine from midnight until eight in the morning. I went to visit him at the mine as he got off work one morning. The sky was the palest blue and the whole world glowed a warm rose color. Soon the sun burst above the horizon and day began. Kee's overburden stripper still had its searchlights on but it was not operating. A bearing had been thrown a few days earlier and it would take almost a week to fix it. He took me on a tour of the three-million-pound machine, whose bucket holds thirty-seven cubic yards. We walked through the inside. "This is as clean as a hospital," he said as he lovingly stroked one of the six engines that drives the shovel. He carefully explained how smaller engines governed larger ones and how they all worked together to lift or drop the line. He told me that being oiler was the most difficult job on the machine because the oiler climbed the derrick while the machine was operating, which was very dangerous. Some men are oilers for fifteen years before they can become operators. Kee was an oiler for two days. He had been trained by Peabody and had caught on quickly to any job he had been given. I looked around at the heaved-up earth and asked him if it bothered him that the Black Mountain was considered a sacred mountain. He answered that for him the coal in the mountain was dead rock, burned rock. For him the mine was a business venture, an income. He felt that many of his people need money badly. He himself has ten children to support, and he felt that nothing was being hurt by removing something dead from the eatrh.

Kee's fascination with machinery had taken him from his traditions and brought him to a place in the white

man's world where he could work and be happy. This mattered more to him than the traditional life he chose to leave. I suppose that when he told me that his people gossiped about success he was really telling me that his people suspected him of being a witch. I remembered Jessie's diffidence about my meeting Kee, and my conversation with him in the pickup.

We climbed up the bucket hoist and examined the inch-and-a-half-thick cable that controlled the scoop. We were perhaps eighty feet above the mine and I could see the sun's warm early morning rays reaching to trees that had not yet perished before the drag line. I turned from the trees and watched the broad proud face of a man who loved a machine. I had divided feelings. I like Kee, but I was not ready to like what the machine was doing. We climbed down and got back in the car, joining my eleven-year-old daughter.

Lindsey's feelings were not so uncertain as mine:

"If they have to have mines, why don't they just put them some place where trees can grow back? Look at those hills. The earth is upside down. Not even the grass can hold there."

As we drove along the wide barren road plowed through to the mine headquarters, the enormous coal trucks coming from other pits rolled along it. They were alien to the mountain, creatures from another planet. Little red lights blinked on them and looked like unbelieving eyes as they lumbered toward their destination, fine black coal dust cascading from their sides.

Jessie and I talked about the mine later.

"The people who destroyed that whole place," she said, "never did ask for the land. They just started moving in without letting all of us know. I would really be upset if I had been raised up there. The land is very important to us around our home because we have to have enough for the livestocks to eat."

She told me of stories that had circulated during the election for Tribal Chairman. The Peabody people, she had heard, were deeply involved in the election.

"People up here think that the mine is a dangerous subject to talk about. If you asked them, they would wonder why you wanted to know. They might get afraid that really you might be here to get information about people speaking against the tribal government. Then they will get in trouble. When you were talking to Mildred Yazzie about it the other day, and she just kept teasing and saying, 'Pee Wee Body Mine—what a silly name for a place to have,' that was because she didn't want to talk to you about it until she knew you.

"A group of guys went up to the mesa to burn the mine down but the Navajo police saw them and ran them off. They had rifles and they were really serious. A lot of people here don't realize what the mines means because they are just so busy surviving. And anyway, there aren't enough people to vote up here for the legislators to care about what goes on. If this was San Francisco—"

The owner of a small restaurant in Kayenta had made a similar remark to me earlier

"Nobody but a handful of Indians knew anything about what was going on up on the mountain before the mine started. We can't get too excited about it. Now, if they started mining down in Monument Valley, which is what brings all the tourists out here, why we'd all be up in arms."

Jessie introduced me to Louise Descheeny, an activist friend and fellow teacher, who gives a class in Native American Studies. Louise had a great deal to say about the mine and whom it would benefit:

"They don't take this into question. They are more concerned about the potential energy. The energy is not even for us. A lot of this electricity is for Los Angeles, Tucson, Phoenix, and who really needs two refrigerators? They don't *need* them, they *want* them.

"We have nothing, no real strong political structure, no big title, no money, no education, no lobbying ability. This type of person can be defeated easily. That's what has happened to the people at Black Mesa. I mean most of those people have probably never even attended chapter meetings where these things are discussed. Most of them don't know what elections are, because it's not part of their life to be standing and voting. The new tribal attitude is to teach them these things so they will know what the issues are. I can't really see this as a future solution because the political machine is very risky to play with. I'm not too sure we will win. We haven't learned to play the game called politics and it's going to take from thirty to fifty years to get really involved in local, state, and national matters and have a respected opinion on issues coming up. This is where the people are not moving fast enough.

"Two groups were invited to go check out Black Mesa a little over a year ago. One group had the complaining citizens—Navajos and others, the other was a group of people chosen to study environmental issues in the area. They had no authority over Black Mesa; they were lobbyist types, used to convince society that there is no pollution, that nothing is really happening up there. Everybody was so impressed and fascinated by the big technological advances—a machine with a big shovel that will hold thirty people. And the pay was appealing. The mine people made it a regular tourist tour.

"When we were coming away from the mine one of the ladies in the tour asked, 'Where is the reseeding going

on?' The man said, 'Right here. We are going through it right now.' The earth was an ugly grayish brown. It looked like sand just turned over. The topsoil was gone. Bottom gravel soil was on top, and it was hard and dry.

"She asked him when they had planted the grass. He said, 'Oh, three years ago. An experimental grass.' But there was no grass and she said so. He said, 'Oh, we're still experimenting.' He was very tense.

"So then we received a great dinner. The press came in and asked the lobbyist types questions. They said there wasn't any pollution. 'We didn't see any dying lambs or dead cattle or angry Navajos. The machines were there, yes, but we don't think they will affect people.'

"They wouldn't interview us. They never gave the Navajos who were opposed to the mine a chance to say anything. They have many ways of swinging the issues like that. So the press sees that there are just a few militant Indians and some environmentalists hollering, but really everything is all right.

"The petitioning to stop the mining died out after that. I went to the hearings. A lot of the local politicians were there. They always show up.

"In the early sixties, we had councilmen who couldn't speak a word of English, and a lot of translators and interpreters. Experts came in and said the land could be mined. They talked about money more than they talked about people. The tragic thing about this is that people are involved.

"One place they thought about moving the Navajos who were in the way of the mine was to Gallup, New Mexico. But the idea died out because the people in that area said they were using the land. Right now the people who are going to be relocated don't have a place to go.

They are sitting in tribal housing in Window Rock. They are being paid either by the Tribe or the government. They don't have a home. They live in trailers in the middle of the fairgrounds.

"What are you going to do with these people? Especially since there is a civic center right next door with a lot of dancing and lots of special activities going on and you have drunks in the area, and burglars?

"You cannot start life all over again because you have no land. Livestock, for instance. You can't raise livestock sitting on the tribal fairground because there's no place to graze them. Of course, you're not getting enough money to buy something that will sustain life for you. You're stuck in a tract that just gives you enough to eat on, and somebody has given you a place to live. It's bare essential living, and that's all.

"Maybe you could house them temporarily, for thirty-five years, somewhere else, then bring them back at the end of the mining lease. But this is the question: How do we know that the corporation will return the land to its original state? Then you ask the risky question: What if they don't return the land to its normal state? Then you can't bring the people back to their home. There's nothing you can do if the land has been destroyed so you have a misplaced people and no future for them."

Louise had not yet finished.

"When people speak against the stripmining on the mountain, one of the statements you hear a lot is, 'The Earth is our Mother.' Then everyone says you're just a romantic militant, that these young people are just looking for trouble. Take that statement, 'The Earth is our Mother.' It means that the earth gives life to us for our survival. It gives life and death. Life means that you are dependent on the local areas, certain places very sacred that are involved in ceremonies. Very sacred means that only certain things are found there. It would not be right for the Navajo tribal government to tear down a church, for instance.

"This is essentially what is happening. The first person to oppose and raise hell would be the preacher. He would say, 'This is the house of God; we pray here.' Navajos say the same thing but they don't say God. They say, The Earth is our Mother.

"A lot of the plants that grow on the mountain are used for medicine purposes. Certain plants grow in certain areas and they are used for very, very sacred ceremonies. When these plants are gone, most times, you just don't do your ceremonies.

"You have to have some ceremonies. I've heard many times where a certain plant is needed for a certain ceremony and a medicine man and driver will drive miles and miles into the mountains without finding it."

ONE DAY, as we walked back to the Whitesheeps' camp, Jessie's friend Lee Kiiyanni explained what the old people had told him about the sacred mountains and The People's strength.

"The Black Mountain is the female mountain and the Lukachukai Mountains are the male. According to my grandmother, it takes male and female to produce any ceremony concerned with natural things.

"Different clans live on different mountains. If we have a light rain, it comes from the female mountain. A heavy rain with thunder and lightning comes from the male mountain."

He alluded then to the mining-company program to drill deep wells for water that could sluice pulverized coal to distant power plants:

"People are concerned with the water level on Black Mesa. They say it is like draining the blood out of the patient. The female mountain is being cut up. It is something like manipulating the body of the whole mountain, and she is being killed. The same thing is happening with the male mountain. Those oil drills are the same thing.

"People who have so much belief worry. If both mountains die, the old prayers and the Navajo way dies. The Navajo people will be dead."

And so too could die the Song of the Earth Spirit:

It is lovely indeed, it is lovely indeed.

I, I am the spirit within the earth.
The feet of the earth are my feet;
The legs of the earth are my legs.

The strength of the earth is my strength;
The thoughts of the earth are my thoughts;
The voice of the earth is my voice.

The feather of the earth is my feather;
All that belongs to the earth belongs to me;
All that surrounds the earth surrounds me.

I, I am the sacred words of the earth.
It is lovely indeed, it is lovely indeed.